SHIFTING STRANDS

SHIFTING STRANDS

Curriculum Theory for a Democratic Age

Bryant Griffith
Texas A&M University – Corpus Christi, USA

SENSE PUBLISHERS
ROTTERDAM/TAIPEI

A C.I.P. record for this book is available from the Library of Congress.

ISBN: 978-94-6209-087-3 (Paperback)
ISBN: 978-94-6209-088-0 (Hardback)
ISBN: 978-94-6209-089-7 (e-book)

Published by: Sense Publishers,
P.O. Box 21858,
3001 AW Rotterdam,
The Netherlands
https://www.sensepublishers.com/

Printed on acid-free paper

TABLE OF CONTENTS

INTRODUCTION

First Thoughts

We knew so much less when I was a child. Then, all I wanted and needed when I learned so painstakingly to read and then to write, was to find a way to be less alone. Which is, of course, what spoken and written language is really all about.

—Philip Schultz

I invite you to begin with me the process of re-conceiving what we call "curriculum theory." Here is the reason. For at least half of the previous century we have battled back and forth about what should be taught in schools, and in the process have been chasing the tail of the variations and permutations of modern capitalist theory. We asked questions like, "Who owns knowledge?" and "How should we maximize time spent in school in relation to cost effectiveness?" and ultimately, "What is the relationship between schooling and the work force?" It is evident by now that there has been no consensus about the answers to these questions. These were valid questions to pose at the time but the epistemological strands have shifted and those questions are now being replaced by different ones, such as, "What does it mean to own knowledge?" and "How much should I share?" and "How do I collaborate with others and maintain my identity?"

All of this is to lay a wreath at the altar of the Roman Goddess Clio. Modern society is ahistorical, acting as though history is of no importance and that the past is simply a story with little or no importance, unless of course it can be "adjusted" to fit a Machiavellian prince (this has been attempted any times). But as our strands shift so do the presuppositions that underlie them, and it is becoming more explicitly clear that the influence of social networks and the subsequent Arab spring are not regional or inconsequential occurrences. Google, Twitter, Facebook, and LinkedIn are more than corporations. They are ideas constructed by fertile minds that are keenly democratic, and new ideas can be revolutionary and paradigm changing. We are entering terra incognito, where there are no linear paths and no fixed addresses, and if you follow me we will work our way through some possibilities by as-ifing—thinking about acting as-if it were the case that something different can happen. This is different than dreaming about a utopia. It has more to do with excavating the artifacts that form our set of presuppositions. That requires that we commit to mastery, purpose, and autonomy in a historical way of thinking about mind, grounded in reflexive self- knowledge. Academically, it's the collapsing of historical and philosophical thinking.

In a time when much academic discourse is saturated with superficial ranks and test scores, I want to present this book as aesthetic discourse and an alternative to the commercial discourse that clouds our skies. I invite you to re-enact your own past and your collective memories. This text addresses the interrelationship of teaching and learning and seeks to capture the complexities of the challenges of teaching and student learning in today's schools. In this text I also focus on a crucial question in education: How does one survive and make changes in a world that seems utterly chaotic? Through this process, this book sketches not just a theory but the outline of a methodology to re-conceive what we do when we teach, learn, and make meaning.

This book argues that we need to attend to the historical and the philosophical so that we can recover what has been done in the past and why, so that we can link the reasons why people thought and acted as they did to our own desires. In this way we can construct non-linear personal stories about ourselves, as a series of on-going "as-ifed" narratives or cautionary tales about truth and life. By striving for community, it becomes possible to construct a tentative sense of shared meaning where we critically respect difference. It is sometimes said that the past repeats itself, but it never really does. We do, however, move in patterns and it is worth the effort to reconstruct those as informative of where we have been and why we chose to act as we did. Self-knowledge and critical reflection have never been luxuries; they are necessary conditions. Today, in our world of personal web-based interactions and access to unimaginable amounts of data schooling needs to reflect and lead. It is time to retool.

This book is designed around three objectives. The first objective is theoretical: to examine how different perspectives of practice and curriculum influence what opportunities are provided to students. Each chapter demonstrates the ways in which teachers can reformulate relationships between teaching and learning in school settings. The second objective is praxis-based: to examine local constructions of knowledge over time and how those constructions are consequential for teacher and student learning. By examining patterns of practice and the processes of knowledge construction in classrooms at all levels and webbing those processes, I lay the foundation for examining commonalities and differences in the construction of knowledge and practices across educational levels, disciplines, and settings. The last objective is to suggest a different lens and an alternate definition of curriculum, and consequently theory.

This is the sixth book I have written in the past six years. I regard these texts as a series of thought pieces, tracing the process of my thinking on topics that have, over time, consumed me. Writing these has been instructive. I have come to truly reflect on my thoughts and the craft of writing. In doing so, I have developed a new understanding of who I am and my need to express my creativity in this way. It would be true to say that I am driven to write. I sit down most mornings, open my computer, and watch in amazement as my ideas flood out in front of me. I offer these to you, my readers, not as seminal works but invitations for a conversation between all of us on our future. I would love to be included in this. I am bryant.griffith@tamucc.edu

MAKING CHANGES HAPPEN IN TERRA INCOGNITA

A Process of Re-enactment

I picked up my *New York Times* on April 20, 2012 and read that Levon Helm had died. I quietly turned to the obituary page and as I read what was written about this man, memories flooded back to me.

The drinking age was twenty-one so we had to sneak in the back door off Yonge Street, Toronto's main drag. It was a seedy section of the street below Bloor then, lined with strip joints and bars, and because of this it was one of places where you could go and hear exciting music in the early sixties. I was there with my friend, John. The two of us were freshly admitted undergraduate students at the University of Waterloo and anxious to make early marks in life. So we became concert promoters. This was a short career because even then concerts were presented by organized thugs and there was no room for amateurs like us.

On one occasion we brought into town a singer who had a number one hit in Canada, Ronnie Hawkins and his band, known then as the Hawks. We got to know Ronnie pretty well and he was kind to us ingénues. About two weeks after the concert we got a phone call from Ronnie's manager inviting us to come into the city and watch the band play for what he called an interview. So, on a Friday afternoon John and I crammed into our friend Ted's Porsche 356 and headed down Highway 401. We parked in the alley behind the bar, knocked on the back door and were let in. Once inside, our escort took us down a flight of stairs to a door that was labeled "Dressing Room" but which really could have and should have been condemned. In the crowded room was the band and Ronnie, center stage talking energetically with a tall skinny kid with a lot of frizzy hair. He introduced us .... Bob Dylan. Dylan had flown in to hear the Hawks at Ronnie's invitation. I knew who Dylan was. I had bought *Free Wheeling* and there was no doubt in my mind that this was a special occasion. Ronnie brought us into the conversation and we sat and talked for what seemed like forever before we all mounted the stairs and the band nervously took their accustomed place near the bar.

Dylan sat alone in a corner. We were all young apart from Hawkins, who deservedly acted as the master of ceremonies. It didn't start well. The band was nervous and there were several mis-takes. They ran though their usual set of Hawkins' favorites and versions of well- known pieces and as it all got going it was clear that something very special was happening. Hours past, Dylan never moved, the bar opened and the usual crowd drifted in and out. The band kept playing, never once looking at the guy with all the hair.

We stayed transfixed for hours but in the late afternoon the bar owner informed us that if we stayed any longer we risked to getting caught as minors and that the bar could lose their license. That magic of that moment is frozen in my mind. Those young men on that little stage in a run-down bar playing with all their hearts. We coasted home, full of beer and excitement. Later, Dylan signed the Hawks and they became The Band. Time passed and John and I never crossed paths with Hawkins again or with any of those no longer innocent youths.

Neal Cassidy (2004), the Beat poet, put it well when he said it was a time when we had no idea of what we would become. The fifties were a time of escape for American youths. Images cascaded across the silver screen, James Dean in *Rebel without a Cause*, Elvis Presley in *Jailhouse Rock*. It was a period of rejecting the austerity of the post-war but with little sense of direction. Even the Beat poets like Kerouac and Snyder expressed a rejection of middle class mores rather than challenging the system. The sixties, however, were a time of great hope. Whereas the Beat generation had no direction home, the hippies directly challenged all facets of American culture and right where it hurt. They didn't want security or traditional jobs or a house in the suburbs. We emerged from the post-war dreariness to a time when everything seemed possible. Instead of coffee houses, poetry and jazz, industrial rock and roll, and sex and drugs became the discourses. These fundamentally challenged the Capitalist structure.

We could conceive of Western civilization simplistically as a static set of presuppositions that held sway over much of Europe from the fall of the Roman Empire until the Renaissance and Reformation, and then the set called the Enlightenment until very recently. This helps us grasp just how difficult change is. It is expedient economically, politically, and socially to believe that one grand narrative exists in perpetuity and one belief system encases it; and it is crucial that in order to maintain the paradigm societies must create institutions to enforce and reinforce it. The extent to which this is brought about often draws the line between popular democracy and autocracy.

There is also a necessary philosophical component to this process. We need to reflect on questions such as the nature of knowledge and if and how it changes. These are not all the questions that need to continuously be addressed but they are imperatives. There are cracks in our epistemological egg, and as they become more and more evident, counter-forces emerge to propel alternatives. One of the major advantages of living in a period of shifting strands is that it becomes more explicit that the presuppositions which once provided us with answers no longer fit. This confusion has not been a major concern in the past because questions about the past and meaning were not pertinent to a populace concerned with day-to-day survival and where access to information and access to knowledge creation were very limited. Today we are at the beginning of a revolution of open access. Each one of you reading this book has the ability to retrieve more data than anyone who lived in the Renaissance. Being able to understand and critically appraise information is no longer a luxury, it is a necessity. Nevertheless, we continue to be more concerned with old paradigm presuppositions like filling seats in schools constitutes learning. What we should attend to is how to critically understand the way that opinion differs from fact in an age dominated increasingly by social media.

We now recognize that the worldview we are abandoning is the imperative created by a prior century of turmoil, not an eternal or universal. As we have uncovered this through a series of stunning scientific breakthroughs and other human endeavors, our sense of confusion and frustrations has grown. The old answers don't fit. Science is often non-linear and theoretical, art doesn't "look" or "sound" like it should (read did), and while we are drawn to change we also long for stability. We long for something that we can believe in, something that links the near past to the amazing present. History demonstrates that a society can survive chaos and complexity for a limited time, but it needs to sense a process toward stability.

The world has continued to shift and its presuppositions have shifted with it. In the past twenty years, the strands have shifted so quickly that it has become apparent to just about everyone that surprisingly dramatic changes are upon us in every imaginable way. However, despite any and all attempts by various power elites to stop or limit this process, the pace of change has gone to warp speed. Today the topic of change is not abstract but concrete and the questions are not "if" and "why," but 'what," "where," and 'when."

Educational theory has been a mirror in this process. Public education was never cast as a social or economic spearhead. It was to serve as a tool to ensure a continued supply of labor and to foster economic growth; and it was assumed that that was good and right. Today, shallow thinking and short-term solutions have sufficiently muddied the waters so that it not clear to the broad populace what the purpose of formal schooling, knowledge, and learning are. So much so, that the question of the merit of wisdom is almost meaningless in our current market-driven, consumer world.

In this terra incognita, teaching and learning need to be recast in light of the growing reliance on social networks. This is best accomplished when teachers recognize that students will learn when they want to and that education is a self-organizing system where learning is an emerging phenomenon. Acting on the belief that teaching and learning are not separate strands but seamless and interconnected, education is transformed from a system of knowledge downloads to one which is an interactive process. As we teach we also learn, and acknowledging this connection opens the door to an educational system that is truly democratic and which is based upon shared expertise.

Speculum Philosophica

I am a speculative philosopher. It's not a title or even a recognized formal group. I know that I belong in this category because as a young graduate student entering into a graduate program in philosophy, with a degree in history, this was a way to describe my way of thinking. I had not realized that this was necessary, but I had a lot to learn and it gave me a focus. Because I was working between two disciplines I fell into an epistemological gap between the two discourses. The philosophy department in which I studied had very specific ideas about what kind of questions could be posed and also very specific ideas about what historians ought to be doing. Categorical thinking like this is often common in academia. I was unaware of this and I found it difficult to learn the discourse of positivist thought.

My career as a learner, teacher, and writer has always been to explore the nature of boundaries and although this was not the first time I had been placed in a box for convenience sake it was one of the more intriguing ones. I liked the sound of this one. You will notice that many of the references I employ in my work are broad and draw from a variety of disciplines. I suspect that there are two reasons for this. First, I was fortunate to be able to spend considerably more time as an undergraduate than most. I moved from university to university in a vagabond type of existence and as a consequence I tried my hand, or I should say my mind, at formal learning in just about every mode of thinking offered. So the palate from which I choose my colors is diverse and my brushstrokes wide. Second, I continue to read widely and I am inspired and draw on what I find to be exciting ideas to which I relate.

Therefore, my speculations are multi-layered and often non-linear and wide. I prefer to think of them as historical re-enactments, a term I learned from reading the work of R. G. Collingwood. So, it is not odd to me that I begin with a question that is not abstract, but comes from my own experiences, namely, "How is it possible to know other persons' thoughts and what happened in the past?" This is a crucial question. In ordinary language we take for granted that we can and do understand one another and that our actions are rational. However, it is far from certain that either of these presuppositions is true and the record of philosophical discourse backs this up. I am not about to enter that discussion, but I do want to provide a provisional suggestion that allows for interaction constructed by understanding in the context of historical understanding. Without such a bridge I cannot sensibly argue for the theory of curriculum that is based on community and cooperation that I propose in this book.

A Prelude in H

I have said that we could learn from the historian's craft, but what is that? Burckhardt (1990) said that history is the story of what one age finds worthy of note in another. Carr (1961) added that it "is a continuous process of interaction between the historian and his facts, an unending dialogue between past and present" (p. 32). Huzinga (1960) claimed that history "is always an imposition from the past and cannot claim to be more. It is always the comprehension and interpretation of a meaning which we look for in the past" (p. 54). Each of these thinkers defined historical thinking as an on-going process between a person in the present and what can be uncovered in the past. I regard myself as being in this tradition.

It could be argued that the past is a collection of texts or documents which contain certain timeless or universal ideas. If this is the case, and I don't think it is, then historical knowledge is a matter of decoding discourse and resetting it in a more contemporary context. In public education we often teach students this and by analogy this is how we know ourselves and the world. But as Quentin Skinner (1978) wrote, this has led to a collection of mythologies which we have mistaken as truths. A second problem with this view is that coherence is often grafted on to a text or action that never existed. I am sure that we all would agree how easy it is to "discover" consistency in our own past actions when at the time they were compulsive. For Skinner and many other social philosophers, the meaning of any action in the past can only be in the range of what was possible for that person. We have to be careful about what we assume was in the mind of the person. Textual interpretation, then, is not a certain way to uncover what happened or why it happened.

Complexity

If this seems complicated that's because it is. I hope to convince you that it is naive and dangerous to take the recorded past as a given. Skinner and the philosophers of his generation were influenced by the work of linguistic philosophers like Austin and Wittgenstein so they turned their attention to how words have been used, and moved away from deductive explanatory models. I cannot stress how important a move this was, not only in historiography, but in thinking in general. The implication was that the recovery of meaning is tied to unearthing the intentions of people and that the methodology is therefore linguistic and understanding because language and its meaning float. This becomes a process of on-going interpretation. I have argued previously that we can extend this methodology to include gestures, dress, and bodily adornments like tattoos. Every picture tells a story and every story has a multiplicity of levels to be considered. I would argue that it is impossible to knit these together and claim that we know what really happened in the past, but we can say that we have an understanding which we are willing to negotiate.

This is what academics do consistently and what seldom happens in schooling. Theories are proposed, discussed, and debated. Often one emerges as dominant and that is taken to be the case, but if we look back over the last two thousand years it is clear that different perspectives, new ideas, and discoveries alter what we take to be truths. My point is that learners know this intuitively and that social networking and the web have reinforced it. Formal schooling too often appears to be a chore, a set of tasks, of memorizing facts that can't be discussed and values that don't seem to have applicability. There is no sense in denying what is happening. Ideas have been set free to be interpreted as they may and too often formal education doesn't offer any solutions. If we want people to understand the importance of the past we have to engage them where they are and help them understand their own motives and intentions. This understanding can be used by analogy to begin the process of knowing others.

Let's consider the work of Collingwood as an illustration of this. In his published and unpublished writing Collingwood claimed that the only way to "know" about oneself and others is to uncover the thoughts of others, in other words, the inside of ideas (Griffith, 1984). Much of modern epistemology has focused on the outside of ideas, the description of an action from an external point of view. What we should be doing is combining both the inside and outside of ideas. This illustrates a presupposition about knowledge, namely that decisions are rarely either/or in nature. In the majority of cases, decisions come about through the negotiation of the inside and outside aspects of the mediating lens of human experience. This process is personal and it is on-going, with the only beginning and end being birth and death. If the experience is historical, in that ideas are re-enacted, then with the intervention of the historian the process is without beginning or end.

Collingwood's work is brilliant and insightful and it represents what Lucretius described as a "swerve," an action with uncharted historical consequences. Greenblatt (2011), in his recent book *Swerve,* chronicled how Lucretius' ideas had on-going yet surprising impacts on the Renaissance and Modernism, despite being suppressed and lost for hundreds of years. I do not regard Lucretius' swerving as an isolated event. History is far more non-linear than it is often painted and one finds what one searches for rather than truths. Facts are selective. This is one reason why historical explanations can be rewritten. Often new evidence is used because the historians are looking for evidence to fit their hypotheses. Collingwood's work follows a similar pattern. Even though Collingwood believed that his writing followed a singular theme, two distinct interpretations have emerged, largely because of the work of T. M. Knox, his executor and the editor of *The Idea of History.* Knox was convinced that Collingwood's later work had become corrupted by the influence of his second wife, a radical thinker by the Oxford standards of the time, and by the on-going consequences of his battle with hypertension, a disease that was then untreatable and eventually led to his death.

Knox saw his role as one of establishing Collingwood's reputation as a major philosophical thinker by constructing a unified body of work from what he considered to be the best of Collingwood's idealist thoughts. Knox regarded much of Collingwood's later work as ill-conceived and out-of-character and he made that case in the "Introduction" to the first edition of *The Idea of History.* This narrative and the subsequent results of the suppression of manuscripts that differed from Knox's view of the "true" Collingwood were not clear until the unpublished manuscripts arrived by parcel past at the Bodleian Library at Oxford on 1979, after the death of Collingwood's wife. Several years later these papers became available to scholars like me, and as the impact of the writings became clear, a general re-assessment of Collingwood and his impact have taken place. Today it is fair to state that Collingwood's swerve impacted much of what we consider to be important about the way historical knowledge and how ideas change over time. Examples of this are Kuhn's work on paradigms and the further work of Collingwood's students like Stephen Toulmin, who widened his influence to scientific thought.

There is much that is dated in Collingwood but if we were to take him at his word, that his work should be built upon, then knowing about the flow of historical ideas becomes a project which swerves into our own transition between modernism and what lies ahead. It informs us about how to teach and learn in the fragmented de-centered world on which we live and in which we strive to construct meaning.

Collingwood was a painter and his family was also artistic. Consequently, he had a great personal interest in the aesthetic. As a painter, archeologist, historian, and philosopher he believed that the artist and spectator jointly come to realize, come to know, certain mental states and that is how meaning is created. The purpose of the historical/philosophical process was to make explicitly clear how human thought could progress to a higher form by clarifying how human actions and historical figures and eras had failed. This process, he argued, could only be accomplished by what he called re-enactment. For my purposes, I want to draw your attention a much overlooked fact, namely the breadth of Collingwood's experience. In his time one strived to be a broadly educated Renaissance man, however today our lens is focused on the specific and on how that relates to obtaining a well-paid job. As a result, we too often lose the broader perspective, the larger brushstrokes.

Collingwood (1946) believed that tracing the history of actions in this way is only possible if there is a developmental process underlying it; a way that presuppositions about an age form, mature, and then lead to a new set of presuppositions. Kuhn (1962) called these sets "paradigms" and his work shows a clear understanding of Collingwood's thought. But what if re-enactment can only uncover the relativity of thoughts? What if it can only uncover what I think now, this second as I write, or tweet? Our social networking age suggests to me that Collingwood's presuppositions were based on the idea that most thinking is rational. Given the pace with which we act today it is safe to argue that we are seldom "careful" thinkers in Collingwood's sense of the word, and perhaps even more importantly we don't value wisdom.

So that we can as-if

Higher education has traditionally been about seeing one's self or thinking of one's self as a member of a specific discourse community. Today this is being criticized as elitist and there is a decided push on both sides of the Atlantic to educate our students in the common discourse of commerce. This is evidenced by the presupposition that all learning should be job-centered and that learning how to be a critical and self-reflective citizen is a useless value. I believe this is a great mistake. The influential leaders of business whom I have met tend to be broadly and well-educated. One could argue that being well-versed in ethics should be considered to be an asset.

Elementary teachers know this, and they have to be multi-disciplinary in theory and practice to cover the curriculum. However, as a child weaves his or her way through the present school system the pressure increases to specialize and to focus on getting a job.

I'm arguing that learning the discourse of a field of study, a discipline, can be and ought to be an exercise in multiplicity and here is why. When we teach we often begin with the premise that the discourse of the discipline is not negotiable. But language, particularly English, is fluid. The rules of usage and the words themselves change and appear quickly. Meaning is tied logically to our words and the way we use them, so it stands to reason that making meaning is also a fluid process. I believe it is also much less linear than we think and what we teach, yet we do understand others and make reasonably good sense of our discourse. So, what is really going on? The answer is that we are constantly engaged in a process I have called as–ifing. We act as-if we are part of a discourse community, picking up signs, metaphors, and decoding until we have sufficient knowledge to understand. In schooling this process often takes about seventeen years, K-16.

We could make this process much more explicit if we were to open it up for negotiation. Why do we not invite students into the process of constructing a formal discourse by teaching them its history? After all, this is what we do with social networking only we generally don't understand that. Perhaps then we could say that our minds are continuously predisposed to construct personal knowledge and to express that in ordinary language.

Re-enacting

Mary Douglas (2007) argued that in Western society we understand because in large part we think in circular patterns. With that in mind, let me return to historiography. Collingwood's lasting accomplishment for me was the pursuit of uniting theory and practice. History is not simply the study of all human accomplishments; it is the study of ideas. It is a story of the development of self-conscious thought in Western civilization.

Historical knowledge is the process of re-enacting the thoughts whose history one is studying. All ideas are part of a complex of ideas and to re-think the past is first to realize that there are two levels of cognition at work: the thoughts in the mind of the person being studied, and the historian's own thoughts. To understand the first it is imperative that we understand the second, because only my knowledge of my own mind can enable me to understand the minds of others past and present. So historical knowledge is the re-enactment of past thoughts encapsulated in a context of present thoughts. On this account, philosophy becomes not just a discipline that is taught or studied as it is often defined; it is the study and development of a process. To study philosophy is to study the process whereby the mind becomes increasingly self-conscious and becomes more involved with particular experiences and not simply with theorizing. We pursue this so that we can see more clearly the situations in which we are called upon to act today. The knowledge of re-enacted past thoughts is self-knowledge and knowledge of the past. Therefore, I can say that I know what a person's thoughts are because I am able to re-think the ideas. This, in turn, leads to a negotiated discussion between my ideas and those of another. The result is my self-knowledge, why I think what I do and this process fuses both teaching and learning. It offers engagement to all involved and invites critical examination without recrimination.

Never slow down.

—Philip Glass

Every reference I have made to thinking is based on the individual's mind. In fact, philosophy is a road map of individual trips into the unknown. However, one of the strands that needs to be unraveled is what can be called "groupthink." Social networking and distance education is centered in collaboration. By its very nature it encourages us to work together and to share. Our contemporary workforce and workplace reinforces this; we often inhabit open spaces in our 9 to 5 existences and form teams which produce consensus results. The idea here is that the group is more powerful than the individual. But is it?

The answer is not always. Cain (2012) wrote that while collaboration is in vogue it may inhibit creativity. Research suggests "that people are more creative when they enjoy privacy and freedom from interruption. And the most spectacularly creative people in many fields are often introverted" (p. 1). The point here is that in this emerging paradigm issues are seldom either/or as they were thought to be in the Industrial age. In the nineteenth and twentieth centuries, we taught that there was a right answer because our world was linear and mechanical. To get it wrong, for example, could be fatal. Today our world is more complex and fragmented, and in case you haven't noticed our decisions are often conditional and relative. If this is true, then we must build in opportunity for both introverted behavior and extroverted behavior, which is just what studies have demonstrated. Our complex and often chaotic world is engaging us in a process which broadens our conception of not just education, but how we think and act. What is driving this are the new technologies associated with the World Wide Web.

Groupthink and the type of collaboration associated with it need to be critically examined and only used when warranted. Teamwork is effective in exchanging ideas, in building understanding and trust, but it can also lead to frustration and hostility. Every experienced teacher knows that group work can be the most complex way to construct learning. It takes time, practice and planning, and in the context I am writing about that means understanding when thinking alone is more appropriate then thinking together. Knowing when to bring the group into collaborative mode is not a matter of time spent on task, but appropriateness based on the participants and the task.

The rules haven't changed; it is just that is apparent that hard work alone or together isn't enough. Intelligence is still a decent predictor of performance, but as Gladwell (2008) pointed out in *Outliers,* practice and hard work are more often the crucial discriminators. In *The Element,* Robinson (2010) described this as a matter of passion. If we aren't passionate about what we do we simply won't shine. If, on the other hand, we are fortunate enough to have the talent, be mentored, or lucky and learn to be persistent, then the sky is truly the limit. It's no longer a straight shot, and perhaps it never was for most people, but in this emerging paradigm it's now explicit. Schooling and how we configure teaching and learning are at the heart of this.

I don't know why we are all here, but I'm pretty sure it's not to enjoy ourselves.

—Ludwig Wittgenstein

This book is not an attempt to re-write or trace the history of philosophy. My choices are subjective and not meant to be taken as anything but that. Having stated this, I cannot leave this discussion without reference to several thinkers and theories which previously and presently impact my arguments. In the process of reading this book you will notice that I will return to these ideas in more specificity. For example, the study of logic has had a dramatic influence on how we see the world and how we teach and learn. Frege (1890) claimed in the early part of the last century that nothing was more objective than the laws of arithmetic, yet at the same time Heisenberg argued quite the opposite. Wittgenstein and others launched a language-conscious century, but the horrors of two world wars rocked our foundational belief in reason and progress and we tended towards the self in phenomenology and existentialism. Husserl (1965) provocatively claimed that "I" exists as mere phenomenon or a philosophical construct. "I" had a voice (p. 231). Lyotard's (1979) post-modernism seemed to cast us further into a world of relativism.

Despite the apparent fragmentation, some basis remains in what has gone before and I believe it is essential for us to ground ourselves and our teaching and learning in the historical/philosophical forms of thought that Collingwood proposed. My argument is that given the time in which we live and the shape and scope of change, we must come to understand that our newly shifting strands are forming a new paradigm, one in which all previous forms of thought are open to all and one in which we each have the opportunity to affect the process.

Which Road to Take?

Where can I begin to map this picture I am painting, this map that can't be drawn without relying on grids, isobars, fronts and lows? Is it possible to open differing discourses to personal stories given voice by the unsaid, the unthought-of, the ineffable? If we put the ideas I've been writing about into a mix and combine them with the spirit of our modern/postmodern post-fragmented world of new learners, then the reframing our curricular and theoretical discourse may well be underway and embodied in the presuppositions of historical/ philosophical thought. This is when I begin to make good on my promise to offer a different definition of curriculum, or at least a different manner to view and think of it.

For the past one hundred years or more, the word "curriculum" has been pinned to two opposing definitions. On one hand, today we live in a positivist world bounded by quantitative charts, high-stakes testing, and bottom-line budgets and funding. In such a world, only accountability based on numbers and test scores counts. Curriculum, on this account, is the explicit or implicit scripted list of memorized facts and figures which "prove" that learning has taken place and that both the teacher and learner have done their job. Opposed to this is progressivism, whose theory is based on thinkers like Dewey and Freire. In general, progressivists have argued that the concept of curriculum encompasses every aspect and action that occurs between teacher and pupil whether inside the classroom, in the hall, or outside the school. Learning has no boundaries. It can make us think, reflect, and act in a reflexive way. Pinar has labeled this the "curriculum war." Curricular discourse is a collection of socially constructed actions which underlie it and frame educational theory and practice. The ways in which these discourses interact is based on our reading the world as a series of texts with no beginning and end. I want to extend this definition of curriculum by suggesting that the borderlines in teaching and learning are permeable and that curricular praxis ought to be widened to include a multiplicity of shapes and forms.

The world has changed. It is increasingly fragmented, de-centered, complex, and often seemingly chaotic. Although it still appears that education is tied to modernism, the slow changes that Kuhn associated with paradigm shifts are increasingly explicit. Despite this, schooling clings tenaciously to the presuppositions of dated conceptions in curriculum practice and theory, as-ifing they could be distinct. It's time to shift those strands. Concepts may be separate but they are not distinct. Modern technology and the web in particular have made this clear. The process is fluid, non-linear, and on-going.

What we are experiencing is an epistemological gap which allows re-drawing the lines, to reframe. Lyotard's (1979) *The Postmodern Condition* is an attack on Habermas' concept of a hermeneutic world, of a transparent and fully communicative society. Lyotard invited us to think about science, society, and history in very different ways by recasting the history and development of ideas in linguistic terms. Reality isn't a matter of mimicking or reproducing facsimiles, it is about how language is used and interpreted. These are intrinsically imperative strands and form some of the most basic presuppositions of this new curriculum theory I am proposing.

Let me push this a bit further. I think of curriculum as a representation of the narratives of the classroom, situated historically and philosophically in re-enactment and self-reflection. This is a multifaceted complex of diversity exemplified in terms of ideology, culture, and language. It is played out in critical reflection both individual and collective in all its forms and permutations. Teaching/ learning and therefore curriculum are not linear. Curriculum is a multi-layered and multi-faceted cautionary tale, open to negotiation. Its influence is only limited by our inability to understand its complexity.

We can see how this could work by considering the hermeneutic thought of Habermas (1989). In hermeneutic theory, teaching and learning are subjective phenomenon and not objective reality, and by linking meaning with the acceptability of speech acts, re-enacting values of reason and freedom a modern curriculum discourse emerges aiming for a pragmatic consensus. The ultimate border crossing for this new curriculum praxis becomes shared experience and the creative power of the mind. Sleeping/dreaming, memory/forgetfulness, compassion/indifference, thought and emotion cloud the border between the here and now. If what is real can be said, then what may or may not be real might be able to be expressed in another form of discourse. It is this sense of fluidity that I am trying to capture, and I suggest that it is the most accurate description of discourse for our times.

Like Wittgenstein, I find it fascinating how well poetry expresses some of our most intricate thoughts. This wider conception of discourse which I have laid out and am stitching together follows this process. I see our borders in both teaching and learning as becoming transparent and even invisible. These are shift changers. The multiplicity of ways in which our students see the world and make sense of it needs to be decoded, but not just as formal speech acts or actions but also in our curriculum, as we teach and learn together.

I argue that all forms of discourse are multimodalities. Most textbooks, curricula, and tests take this form. When discourse is made explicit through strategic story-telling, teaching and learning can become transparent, where both teachers and students are acknowledging others' voices. When detours arise in discourse they open the door to a curriculum of this type. Decoding discourse together in our day-to-day activities is a way of looking at our multidimensional, transnational, intercultural world. In our case, I hope that individual actions are made in the context of classrooms where interpretive narratives are cautionary tales. These stories are the "as-ifing" scenarios about what we are learning. They are works in process and in progress. They are construction zones where the boundaries are fluid and where it is permitted to take a chance.

An Example

Digital storytelling enables individuals and communities to reclaim their personal cultures. It is a cautionary example of framing common discourse. Digital story is also a curriculum tool, in the way that I frame the concept, for shaping cautionary tales and cultural narratives. This is because it is offered in a digital context in which many learners may feel comfortable, unlike most other learning formats which are presented in a set manner. It invites both teachers and learners to think and create new types of communication outside the realm of traditional linear narratives.

Digital storytelling also presents opportunities for learners to de-construct their present frame work and reconstruct one that fits their own context. It engages students in the praxis of what I have been describing in this book and it fits with what researchers "see" when they apply action research methodology. In other words, it makes explicit my sense of curriculum by collapsing theory and practice within the historical and philosophical theory I have previously described.

Engaging teachers and learners in this way tells us explicitly through our actions that there can be a discussion, a conversation, about methods, about means and ends. It doesn't imply irrationality or relativism. This isn't a dialectic, an either/or situation. It is an active, on-going interchange between teacher and learner about possibilities in which individual opinions can be presented, reflected upon and then critically examined from individually supported viewpoints. The difference in this approach is that each position and idea is acknowledged as a possibility, not as a truth or fact. There is no necessary progression from one set of ideas about something to the next unless there is agreement, and even then any series of ideas is "in process."

This is the way the thinkers in the history of ideas look at the world. They might say that historical epochs or ages are defined by historians after the fact. After all, no one knew they were living in the Middle Ages at the time. What were they in the middle of? At one point, the same time period was called The Dark Ages. Whose idea was that? Labeling may help people in the present make sense of the past and see it as an historical progression, but we mapped it out. We named it. Historians know this. It's not news but if it is presented as fact in school, if the textbook presents it as fact, and if school boards test knowledge on this premise, we are giving learners a dangerously superficial view of our world. One might argue that to teach that the world is far more complex than students can comprehend is the only way public schooling can exist, it fails as soon as any one of us opens their web browser.

And so to Praxis what we Believe

Collingwood (1946) argued that the highest state of mankind was one in which all discourse (my word) was reflective and explicit. He saw this as the collapsing of historical and philosophical thought and action. It is hard to do this, and too often we have been side-tracked by dictators or those seeking easy and quick solutions, but today we can really attempt this in the gap we live in. Education is a process in which both real guides to the landscape and those that create imaginative confusion are required. This is a balancing act deeply rooted in the multiplicity of our discourses.

We can learn how to do this by attending to other fields like anthropology, history, and literary theory. In this process, we need to acknowledge, and often become, liminal teachers and learners. We do this by "as-ifing," recognizing boundaries are fluid, becoming heteronymous, and by rejecting colonialist mimicry and surveillance. This is about storytelling.

Our narratology can be a series of possibilities as well as sites of resistance, all constructed in discourse communities. These communities are represented by explicit, praxis- based discourse which is social in character. In these contexts, both teaching and learning are not limited by place or by the hours in a school day. It is possible for us to create schools that are labs for cooperation. They would be multilayered and fractured, and torn open by the pressures of our modern/postmodern society.

MEDIATING THE COMPLEXITY OF TEACHING AND LEARNING

Self-knowledge is kind of funny thing because the less you have of it you have, the more you think you have. You see, that's it's a twisted blessing. When I was 22 or 23 I had … self-knowledge but I lost it along the way somewhere … I think it's hard to lose your old habits, even the ones that have led you wrong or come close to killing you.

—Bruce Springsteen

SHIFTING

Does this sound familiar? I am going to make your life better but change everything you are comfortable with, and we'll do this with new technologies, less money, and more high stakes testing for which you are accountable. The problem is you can't refuse, so you try your very best to understand what it is you need to do and still accomplish what you want to do in the classroom. But you can't. Politicians, school administrators, parents, students, and your colleagues are all on different pages. It's as though you missed a meeting. Here is the good news. You aren't alone. Extremely rapid change has engulfed all of us and separated us from the familiar. The complexity of academic discourse and knowledge construction points to the need for us to examine how teaching is interdependent with student learning. I think this is a philosophical issue that can be made personal and one which has a solution that you can adapt to your own needs. Let's begin with a reflection and a cautionary tale.

For every story there is a beautiful journey.

—Francis Ford Coppola

In Schultz's (2011) book titled *My Dyslexia*, he painfully describes in hindsight his early life as a dyslexic child. My experiences are similar in many ways. I don't recall there being a connection between being taught to read and to write. I remember phonics, recitation, repetition, flash cards, and testing. It's a blur. I also recall having my left hand hit on numerous occasions until I learned to write with my right hand. I wish I could blame my handwriting on this but I can't. I was taught that writing was a physical skill whose only connection to reading was to fill in the correct answer in my work booklet.

I think it was blue and about five by eight inches. I often had to draw in the lines myself, as a measure of good writing was to be able to write in straight lines without such aids. Like Schultz, I was perceived as stupid and largely ignored. In grades seven and eight I was placed in the back of the classroom. I was given a stack of paper from which I was free to construct paper airplanes which I was permitted to throw out the window. I could not read for understanding or tell my left from my right. I was unable to understand what was being asked of me or said to me.

I have always had school-sickness, as others have sea-sickness. I cried when it was time to go back to school long after I was old enough to be ashamed of such behavior.

> Still today, I cannot cross the threshold of a teaching institution without physical symptoms, in my chest and my stomach, of discomfort or anxiety. And yet I have never left school.

—Jacques Derrida

This I believe accounts for my reputation as a troublemaker at school and at home. I memorized sounds, words, and the alphabet. I did it myself. Even today, I have to begin at the letter A to re-discover the sequence of the alphabet and when put under pressure by a type "A" personality, I often lapse back into confusion and panic. Learning to read and to write were skills I acquired despite schooling. I was read to at home and in the local public library, but I lived for my imagined life and voice from comic books. It was through this genre that I discovered syntax and the colorful pictures helped me to make sense of the words in the bubbles that floated above the action figures heads. I was able to do this in two ways. Initially, my make-believe world was puppet characters made out of tiny cereal boxes. Every Saturday morning I would stage a puppet performance in the children's section of our local library. In order to accomplish this I had to work up a script and in this manner I was able to put into words the voices of my characters.

The second way was to transform myself into a super hero. In the 1950s Saturday matinees usually featured two short action serials. Some of my heroes were cowboys but my favorite was Batman. I had borrowed one of my mother's old sheets and cut it into the rough shape of a bat cape. This I hid under my shirt but when my alter ego appeared on the screen, I unfurled my cape and ran wildly about the theater. Why I was never caught I do not understand. By becoming a super hero I was able to make sense of the spoken language on screen. Years later, I was able to make the magical transformation to written language. As I became older, I memorized the craft that the authors of the books I was reading employed. More than anything else I was determined. I had heard that Winston Churchill had learned to write this way, but his books were far beyond anything I could mimic. What I could do was to read copiously and widely. I began to concentrate on the field of history, and in Gladwell-time (a reference to the "10,000-hour rule" of skill mastery from Gladwell's (2008) text, *Outliers: The Story of Success*), I learned the basics of the art. Through the years I struggled on, determined, and the maverick in me uncovered several key artifacts: creativity, a good ear for music, and an excellent memory. I made it.

Artifacts

My research has focused on multicultural settings inside and outside schools where the maverick nature is tied to culture and language, as well as to the stories of mavericks who have become successful despite their school experiences. In each case, a type of pedagogical model has emerged where concepts and ideas weave and intertwine as teachers and learners together explore and shape shared and personal meaning. In this way, each teacher and learner implicitly or explicitly uncovers his or her "self" and the "self" of the other. When sufficient numbers of people coalesce around a topic, to oppose the dominant culture, to remember their cultural stories, and to imagine a future toward which they are prepared to work, then change can happen. These spaces are sites of resistance. This is an epistemological framework rather than a directly observed phenomenon, that I have called as-ifing. It inhabits the gaps where discourse is fluid and negotiable and where there is a conscious attempt to attend to relevant cultural matters, especially those associated with ideology and power structures.

All culture is a story with multiple authors, sometimes it is implicit and at other times it is explicit. To make sense in this complex and chaotic world we need to construct a different consciousness to transform society into one that is inclusive. One can understand this through the actions of mavericks. Postmodern critical theorists would argue that educators need to fully acknowledge and work with teachers, parents, and students where they are. Being situated in the fluidity of the here and now helps to recognize the importance of communities and grassroots movements in education. These grassroots education movements can be fundamental to bringing everyone back into the education equation. As postmodern critical educators, we cannot afford to passively sit by and watch the debate over the future of education. We need to create the conditions for students to become critical agents in the on-going process of social transformation.

From my perspective, a vibrant, relevant, effective critical pedagogy must be simultaneously intellectually rigorous and accessible to multiple audiences in multiple forms and on multiple levels. I cannot think authentically unless others think. I cannot think for others or without other.

Sifting and Blurring

In my world of praxis, boundaries are blurred, fused, or bleed into one another. I see differences in discourse as distinct but not separate. While I continue to point out how these various strands of intellectual thought can be placed together to form meaning, their pattern more often than not appears. In reality though these are emerging concepts, and their meaning is to be discovered through reflection and the historical process. So please take this opportunity to become Indiana Jones and excavate your intellectual artifacts in an informed ways that fits your unique and individual context.

One reason we can re-imagine the world of education in which teaching and learning are negotiable is that both teachers and students are no longer certain about what it means to be an "expert." Said (1994) argued that the idea of "expert" implies a privileged opinion of control. I have suggested to you that in this modern/postmodern world that we are rejecting the notion that ideas and concepts belong to or are owned by particular groups. We deny any "drift" towards consolidated power and authority and we embrace individual liminal voices, often because we have to. How else can we uncover understanding? In short, we are setting sail from our safe harbors without a map, but with a purpose.

Moreman (1988), in his book *Talking Culture*, argued that "social interaction is the overwhelmingly preponderant locus and the form in which culture and society are learned, enforced, and manipulated" (p. 21). We need to think about discourse in terms of the identity it helps shape. Identity and sameness are interrelated. When we claim a personal identity we also claim identity with a group Whatever rituals we establish, whatever myths we live by, all educators will not be alike any more than all students, so we can't paint ourselves back into the box where we were a hundred years ago. Ours is a fragmented world of possibility bounded and framed by cultural discourse, so our studies, like ourselves, must be fluid. All of this is an on-going process of intersecting concepts that fuse and deconstruct and then reconstruct through the explicit action of our discourse.

Flashing-back

I sat alone in the big auditorium. Everyone else in ninth grade had been assigned to a homeroom and had a class schedule. It looked like I didn't make it into high school. I was to go to trade school. Then, through the intervention of my parents I was allowed to attend and I managed to pass grades nine and ten. But in grade eleven things fell apart. I sat in the front row of my Algebra class because I was put there. The teacher had parabolic mirrors on both corners of the front boards so he could keep a watchful eye on us as he scribbled on the board. On one of these fateful occasions, he reeled around and asked me exactly what I was doing. My answer was that I was trying to make sense, to understand what he was talking about. His answer was that I should stop trying to understand and to just do was I was told to do. The subtext, later stated explicitly to me, was that nothing I learned in that class had anything to do with my life outside his classroom. Although my grade that year was something like 23%, I quickly learned what I needed to do to succeed in school. It's a lesson that I still sometimes follow. The point is I now knew there was a road map and how to follow it.

Historiographies

Today there doesn't appear to be a road map and that suits my mind. We live in a fragmented world where our cultural discourses are as varied as our voices. It seems that the social contract that has bound us together for hundreds of years had broken down into multiple discourse communities based upon self-interest, and it is in this framework that those of us living in the world of education inhabit.

There are several ways to approach this. One path is to unquestioningly do as you are told and become a scripted lesson, or to put it another way, to be compliant. I don't suggest you do this, as it often leads to an even more confusing conversation with yourself. Another possible path is to get out of the classroom and to choose a different career. Unfortunately, many highly gifted people see no hope for themselves in this profession and opt out. I regard this as a tragedy. Then, there is you. If you had chosen either of the two previous options you wouldn't be reading this book. So, what's to be done?

It is worth our time to consider why this is so and how we might construct both personal and shared understanding. In very broad and sweeping terms, Western philosophy has used the debate between Plato and Aristotle as its crucible. Knowing "what" and "how," and knowing what constitutes sufficient conditions for proof, has revolved around the same presuppositions for almost two thousand years. But to address the various epistemological strands that comprise teaching and learning and to sift through them in such a way as to make sense and clarify, it is necessary to recognize that the world has shifted, fragmented, and slid in such a way that the grand narrative is no longer recognizable. Instead, we inhabit a world in which all opinions are self-referenced and where the common good is not a factor. In this context, it is fair and meaningful to inquire about what it means to teach and to learn. In our world, the very nature of language is continually in process and the rapid use of new technologies, words, and concepts bleed into one another to the extent that we feel there is no root meaning. It is easy to feel powerless and lost. The sociologist Durkheim (1922) called this anomie. Anomie means there is a lack of social norms or a sense of normlessness for an individual or group. Durkheim used this term to describe the breakdown of social norms and it has been adapted by thinkers like Herbert Marcus and many others. Today I believe that we are again in a period of intense anomie, particularly among those of us involved in schooling. Like the inhabitants of the nineteenth century, we suffer from a perceived mismatch between our personal and group standards and the wider social standards of the time. And like the nineteenth century, the causes are rooted in rapid change.

In the last decades of the twentieth century the nature of the conversation has changed in a dramatic manner. What constituted the canon of thought has come under assault, as has the structure of the thinking that lay behind it. In other words, the presuppositions on which we have based our thoughts about our world since the Enlightenment, or modernism, are being attacked. Public education as we know it began in the late eighteenth or early nineteenth century and it was modeled on the needs of the time. This was a time where there was a rapidly expanding population in an emerging industrial age. Historians often call this the Enlightenment. It presupposed that hard work ensured success and that progress entailed human mastery of nature. Schooling became the tool of the Enlightenment. It initially trained people to become industrious agricultural workers, and then as complex factory cities emerged, schools retrained the youth to become good assembly-line workers, "little boxes" as Woody Guthrie once described them. What it didn't do was teach people to be independent thinkers. That makes sense, doesn't it? No one wanted an automobile assembly-line worker to re-think the design of the car door he was attaching while he was at work. That would slow the assembly and have an effect on productivity. The goal was to create a class of workers who were compliant and hardworking. Schooling mirrored those values. In fact, it still does.

Then, the twentieth century brought wave upon wave of change. We became wealthy, powerful, and personally independent and schooling often just got in the way. We found that television brought us new and exciting ideas and that the concept of deconstruction appeared to tell us that it was permissible to make up our own minds about what was true and real. However, schooling kept the same script that the only way to be successful was to follow the rules and stay on track for as long as possible. The more education the better and education was to be of a particular kind, academic. This isn't as sinister as it might sound. Learning to read, write, and think rationally and in a reflective manner are, I would argue, some of the essential building blocks of democracy, but we lose many of the people who could possibly bring new and creative ideas into the mix. These students often opt out to careers in the world of work, before business school and pursue career in the entertainment field or professional sports. As a result we have witnessed a flowering in these fields.

Towards the end of the twentieth century, the internet radically changed the equation. It became possible to get a university degree without sitting in a classroom and it could be done in your choice of place and time. Students became faceless; gender, ethnicity, and social status became opaque if not invisible. The introduction of Google, Wikipedia, Facebook, Twitter, and many others tipped the balance and changed the narrative forever. Schools and teachers no longer owned knowledge and further, what constituted knowledge was unclear, if not meaningless. Schooling responded by shutting off the conversation and prescribing a curriculum comprised of subject- specific facts and sets of questions which, when answered correctly on high stakes tests, constituted success. Students responded by leaving their minds at the entrance to the classroom.

Choosing to Re-enact

The period often called the Enlightenment, which Wikipedia correctly informs us was "an elite cultural movement of intellectuals in 18th century Europe, sought to mobilize the power of reason in order to reform society and advance knowledge. It promoted intellectual interchange and opposed intolerance and abuses in Church and state." The Enlightenment flourished from about 1650 until about 1800. Immanuel Kant was one the philosophers who formulated this view. According to Kant, the Enlightenment was the emancipation of the human consciousness from states of ignorance and mistake. This was the age of reason, of progress, egalitarianism, and common concern. Chartier (1989) said: "This movement [from the intellectual to the cultural/social] implies casting doubt on two ideas: first, that practices can be deduced from the discourses that authorize or justify them; second, that it is possible to translate into the terms of an explicit ideology the latent meaning of social mechanisms" (p. 39).

Our view of education as rational, critical, and an open discussion of public issues is based on this and so is our conception of democracy; so, when I argue that these presuppositions are under attack it implies an end to a grand paradigm. There are many reasons for this: the movement of peoples, the development of international trade and commerce, and the changes and questions to the Enlightenment's core beliefs by and through the open dissemination of materials through the web and the open discussions introduced by social media. The sketch I have been drawing in this chapter is about exactly this. Formal schooling itself and all its entailments like how we teach and learn are based in the Enlightenment. We need to understand this and how to adapt to an emerging paradigm in order to preserve what is appropriate and to make that meaningful in a new context.

The concern for rational discussion, for openness, and for egalitarianism calls for choices to be made and the ability to make decisions. We all make decisions and we make them all the time, but often why we do is confusing because the ground if shifting. We're shifting the sands, where in the Enlightenment they were static and taken for granted. It may seem that we are all losing control of our lives, but the reality is that never before has a generation had to make so many choices all the time.

To Decide…or Not

I carry an iPhone, have an iPad, and listen to music in different modes, one of which is an iPod. I also write on a computer. On innumerable occasions every day I make decisions about whether or not to accept, ignore, or make a phone call, a text, or an email. This might not seem like a big thing but it intrudes into what I am trying to accomplish in terms of work or play on a daily basis. When educators teach, they choose when to begin, how to proceed, in what order, who to call on when a question is asked, and so on. Learners choose to attend to the lesson or not, to what extent, what to filter out as unimportant, as well as the numerous social decisions related to being in a learning environment. And then there are big decisions about morality.

Without a doubt, we make more decisions that impact our lives every day than ever before and the truth of the matter is that we burn out. Baumeister and Tierney (2011) called this "decision fatigue" and they argued that self-control is the key. Making decisions is tiring and they deplete one's will power. According to these authors, "When the brain's regulatory powers weaken, frustrations seem more irritating than usual. Impulses to eat, drink, spend, and say stupid things feel more powerful" (p. 46). Good decision making, they argued, is a state of fluctuation, so in this chapter and the following let's begin to collaborate on ways to increase our ability to make decisions about teaching and learning in this decentered, fragmented, and complex world.

Threading: The Positivist Sense of "Problem"

It is important to understand why multiple literacies, are important in the context of mavericks and maverickness. I don't regard this as a presupposition or strand. It's more of a thread, an idea, or a concept. Let's follow this.

In the era of modernism, roughly from the eighteenth century until the near present, positivism has been one of the most prevalent and persistent forms of academic discourse. While much of the learned world embraced positivism, education has remained, to some extent, an area of field-based study. The public view of education has often been one of a failed and out-of-touch system. Attempts have been made to make educational systems more relevant by imposing national testing and national curriculums. Positivism claims that the scientific method could and should be applied to understand human interactions both in the past and in the present. Understanding can be developed through the simple process of observation, categorization, and labeling, and this leads to the discovery of another law of human interaction and behavior. This has been called the Newtonian World- Machine. It holds that the entire universe acts according to basic laws, which are everywhere and always the same. The laws exist and all that humans have to do is discover them.

The pedagogical model which follows positivism is often one based on rote learning and rule following. It has been characterized as "the just in case" model, which means that students learn so-called facts just in case they may need to recall them as some point. While this model may have some merit in a Fordist factory model it has little application to the contemporary world.

Fordism and Post-Fordism as Problematic Threads

Fordism is a manifestation of positivist thinking and takes its name from the production techniques developed by Henry Ford. It presupposes economies of scale and supply driven production. Thus, the more that can be supplied the lower the cost to the consumer, who will then purchase that which was produced. The workers in turn are protected by trade unions and state intervention. Therefore, the state's role in the capitalist economy was established. As key components of the economy followed Ford's lead, the welfare state was born. Public education followed the Fordist model. There was no room for the mavericks. If they succeeded it was because of luck or the intervention of a mentor. Schools were organized into grades with defined learning expectations and outcomes. Teachers were certified to provide quality assurance as children were required by law to attend school.

This system worked as long as the graduates of public education became consumers and adhered to the presuppositions of modernism, especially the idea of progress and consumption. The entire system was also predicated on one form of textuality, the written text. It was essential in Fordism that workers follow instructions to keep the wheels of industry moving smoothly; therefore, more traditional forms of understanding such as oral histories were shunned. The public was encouraged to read narratives which reflected modernist goals and to stay away from the bottomless pit of relativism as found in areas such as autobiography. It was felt that smart people were those who read the appropriate texts and followed the canon, a canon which was largely European, white, and male. Of course these views were not held nor widely promoted by institutions of higher learning. As a result, an increasingly wider gap grew between the literacy haves, those who discern the meanings of text, and the have-nots, those who were not privileged to receive such an education. For most learners, it is the personal small stories of their lives which make meaning and construct their horizons. And it is in this world that the sense of learning which incorporates narrative and multi-textuality addresses.

Strands of Positivism, Deconstruction, and Paradigms

Positivism is a strand for me. It is a philosophical principle that underlies a great deal of western civilization in the last three hundred years. It has not been altogether successful in our schools. The influence of Dewey, Freire, Eisner, and Gardner, to name a few, have strengthened the latest round of mostly politically-based attacks on both the nature of schooling and the system which gave it birth. Yet philosophically the attacks on positivism have been relentless and on-going. Two examples of this are the concept of deconstruction developed by Derrida (1979) and the concept of paradigms and paradigm shifts introduced by Kuhn (1962). I stress these two because in both cases they have been largely misunderstood by educators.

Deconstruction and the concept of paradigms allow for the opportunity to address the learning style of mavericks. As such, I regard them as presuppositions of our emerging view of self and the world. Yet they aren't of the same order as positivism, which is itself a world view. Derrida's use of deconstruction has very little to do with the destruction of culture or moral relativism. Instead, it refers to what is signified when we speak a word. For example, the word "dog" signifies a four-legged animal which barks, scratches, and so on. Derrida (1975) argued that the meaning of words is not conceptually or materially obvious. So, to know the meaning of the word "dog" we would need to know what type of dog. Making meaning of words, for Derrida, is a matter of contextual mapping.

In a wider and more popular sense, or in common language, deconstruction plays itself out in everyday speech in the way that most meaning has become relative to a speaker's context. It is unfair and untrue to argue that this broader sense of the term is wrong because it has so pervaded contemporary thought. It is simply the case, rightly or wrongly, that for many people in Western society the meanings of words and concepts shift with the context to which they are applied. In today's schools, the concept of deconstruction has taken on a broader and even less structured meaning. Students see their world as deconstructed and fragmented through modern technologies and they have come to view themselves in a strictly relativistic sense. Their visuals, their music, their stories, and therefore their desires, motivate them. Everything is relative to them. In this world, teaching and learning have a key role to play because they are based upon the necessity of honoring prior experience, the construction of knowledge, and the role of narrative in self-knowledge. In essence, it speaks to the maverick in all of us but in particular those among us who walk a different path or discover the world in a divergent way.

The "Problem" Appears to Shift Further

In 1962, Kuhn published one of the most significant books of the twentieth century. In *The Structure of Scientific Revolutions,* Kuhn argued that science is not a steady, cumulative body of knowledge but a series of events linked by common presuppositions, or a paradigm. It is also punctuated by intellectually violent revolutions. After such revolutions, one conceptual world view or paradigm is replaced by another. For Kuhn, the history of science is a pattern of common ideas being accepted as defining an age and then followed by a revolutionary type of change. This view clashed with the Enlightenment's view that knowledge was the steady progressive path to a better world. It also provides a justification for including what are often labeled non-traditional curricular models like problem- based learning in our curriculum.

In popular thinking, or common language, a paradigm has come to be synonymous with any structure of ideas that one holds. To the best of our knowledge Kuhn never applied his work or intended to apply his work to broad social change. Nevertheless, like the case of deconstruction, the meaning of Kuhn's concepts has been taken to mean that the relativist views about the world one holds can form a paradigm or belief structure and that deconstruction might be the process one uses to make sense of the world. If, as I suggest, the epistemological ground can shift, we should think of teaching and learning as small narratives that connecting our world.

Every act of creation is first an act of destruction.

—Pablo Picasso

If there is an emerging paradigm, it can be described by using the discourse of postmodern critical theory described by thinkers like Lindof and Taylor (2002). This is terra incognita. What was originally a geographic term used by cartographers to fill in the spaces or un-named regions is now used to metaphorically to mean any unknown subject or field of research. I see my thinking and writing as an example of this. I have written and argued that in quantum mechanics, the world exists "as-if" it was the case that "x" was the case and that those that we label as mavericks implicitly regard it this way as well. Mavericks like Picasso, Miles Davis, and Banksy presupposed that ideas are in constant flux and in process. If we think of this in terms of as-ifing, then the concept of "maverickness" might further presuppose the world to be this way in order to function in it and make provisional sense. In *School Stories,* (Rose & Griffith, 2003) the narrators have all constructed their worlds "as-if" it was the case that the rest of the world are in agreement. Often, in fact in most cases, it is not this way and it is this type of divergent thinking that causes mavericks to disconnect from formal education and even the outside world. Narratives, personal or shared, whether implicitly or explicitly stated offer a solution in that they invite learners to interact with other learners and with teachers in framing the way in which they learn. It is in this way that teaching and learning fuse and collapse, distinct but not separate.

I've come to realize through my writing that I have an epistemological absolute presupposition and it is that our cultural narrations, our discourses, must be imbedded in our reflexive practice. This is more than praxis itself, the direct application of theory to practice. For me, reflexive praxis is a process without beginning or end which demands that I think about what I am thinking in the context of my discourse community. I inhabit this "as-if" world thinking that I can decode, deconstruct, construct, and reconstruct multiple discourses with the possibility of negotiating some form of understanding. I'm not making a knowledge claim here. I'm talking about something that is in some way phenomenological in character. That is, as stated in *The Shorter Routledge Encyclopedia of Philosophy,* where "subjects and objects are interrelated" (p. 791). In other words, understanding is problematic and descriptive, like mid-level research. But for me, this process is grounded in a way of understanding history as having sets of historically real presuppositions which can be traced and given relative meaning. It's a tricky line between realism and skepticism, but it's how I have made meaning of my world.

Posing questions and constructing knowledge based upon prior experiences creates the opportunity to build a different type of social capital, one based on diversity within the structure of what must be learned in formal education. In this way, mavericks can lead the way for us as we examine our sense of curriculum and the learners who live it. It seems that this is what many students do in school. They do not believe that the world is unchangeable but instead make sense of it as if it were. This allows students to make sense of standard based positivist curriculums without the fear of losing their sense of deconstruction. How much better it would be to consider teaching and learning as a continuous process, always under construction and conditional.

Perceived links

Taken alone, in a different time, Derrida's and Kuhn's thoughts might not have made the impact they did. However, the attack on the presuppositions of the modern world proceeded in a different way than such attacks in the past. The essential presuppositions of this neo-modernism were adopted in a non-rational way. Once it appeared that deconstruction undercut what seemed to be the necessary and sufficient link between what is referenced and its object, general meaning could be separated from specific meaning and a whole range of consequences emerged. For example, post- modernists might suggest that it is not possible to share meaning in a large national sense.

It is to this new world that the ideas of both Derrida and Kuhn have been adapted. If success depends upon flexibility, then traditional schooling fails because students spend far too much time thinking about why people act and about the long term consequences of actions. In other words, it is believed that students spend far too much time on theory rather than practice. Implicit in this attack on modern education is the questioning of the value of many academic disciplines. For example, if practice is a present problem that is unrelated to the past, of what value is the study of this theory? Likewise, if literacy calls for complex levels of interaction between the reader and the text, why learn literary theory? Put in another way: why not equate literacy to phonics?

If one were to couple this with the development of information technology then learners become consumers and education becomes a ticket to a flexible job market, one where the worker is offered no tenure and no assurances of job protection. In this post-Fordist world learning becomes matter of reading the text to get on with the job (Jessop, 2002). To a modernist this seems to be similar to learning how to understand a car manual or install a new electronic device in their home, and it is. In the post-Fordist world there just isn't any time or need for the intricacies and intellectual interlacing of ideas (Tremblay, 1995). Kuhn and others provide a venue for us to consider differing conceptions of education as an opportunity to widen the narrow conception of teaching and learning implicit within post-Fordism (Mishra, 1990). There are distinct differences in the way humans perceive situations and confront problems; particularly in the relationship between the learning styles of students we call mavericks and the learning styles of more traditional learners. It is my view that in order to understand how we teach and learn it is necessary to contextualize the discourse of multi-textuality, and to link narratives, to place, and a sense of a deconstructed self.

Tell me a Story

Autobiographical texts appear to make explicit what I have laid out in this chapter. Today, they are able to make explicit and to help decode what has previously been a subtext and implicit. They give voice, and in the process question what have been called historical presuppositions about what we believe is the basis for the way we view the world. One example might be that narratives question the ability of the public school system to fully prepare children for life in a vibrant democracy. These autobiographical texts are not simply bourgeois individualism. Like Connelly and Clendenin (1989), these stories represent personal, practical knowledge of how to get by without succeeding in school. They tell us of how students succeed despite the myths of how to behave and learn in our society.

Here's an idea. Let's re-frame teaching and learning to fit the needs of this rapidly emerging paradigm and the students who are growing up defining it, because in case you haven't noticed that is exactly what Wikipedia has done. One way to begin is to re-cast what is currently labeled as product and view both teaching and learning as a process, which by the way it is more often than not. And it's also non-linear. Historically, Western civilization has transmitted shared knowledge in circular terms through oral and written discourse. If we continue to disregard what I would argue is an historical presupposition, we risk losing an historical footprint. Reconstruction could begin by concentrating on what each of us does well, or as Hawking (2011) put it, concentrate "on things your disability doesn't prevent you doing well" (p. D1). We can reframe our talents and abilities in terms of what we can do and not what we lack or may be unable to do. After all, success is often intangible and at least as much a matter of spirit and outlook as it is about test scores.

Making a shift like this is thinking "as-if" learning is a series of mis-takes and not mistakes. The same can be said of teaching. Our capitalist world is driven by the desire never to be wrong and being wrong is considered to be disastrous; but in the real world of life experience, we learn by doing. If we add reflection to the equation learning becomes a continuous series of interactions between teacher and learner in and by which both propose and consider beliefs and knowledge, and then react on the basis of prior knowledge and experience. The result of such a process is both personal and shared knowledge conceived through negotiation, deconstruction, and reconstruction.

We Share

Shared knowledge, like a scientific theory, can have a longer shelf life, but personal knowledge floats. Increasingly it is tied to place, time, and immediate context. Education in its widest sense needs to clarify this because it's not immediately clear to anyone outside of researchers. Well, that's not quite true because many teens and pre-teens get the idea, but in a similar way that deconstruction is sometimes interpreted as making your own meaning. We, as teachers, need to take a collaborative lead and negotiate with learners based on where they are not where we want them to be. Remember it's a process that has loops and curves, not a straight line.

Let's reframe again. Critical theory is a methodology that concerns itself with "forms of authority and injustice that accompanied the evolution of industrial and corporate capitalism as a political-economic system" (Lindof & Taylor, 2002, p. 52). I've been arguing for the last five years that we are living in a fragmented, decentered, and emerging paradigm that is far different and not yet explicit. If we think of critical theory through the lens of postmodernism actions, problems become situated "in historical and cultural contexts, to implicate themselves in the process of collecting and analyzing data, and to revitalize their findings" (Lindof &Taylor, 2002, p. 52). Viewed from this perspective, making meaning is non-linear and is relative to the context of social structures and place becomes a major driver.

In the past, educational research has taken it as a given that its research is objective and that motives and intentions are on-going. Lindof and Taylor, among others, point to a perspective that is multi-faceted and situated in contexts that are fragmented, decentered, and continually in flux. This postmodern twist presupposes that both the researcher and the subject are reflective collaborators.

Both Lindof and Taylor are anthropological ethnographers, and in the past there has been a considerable transference of ideas between anthropology and disciplines like history and philosophy, for example, the work of R. G. Collingwood. My aim, as always, is to bring these connections and ideas to the surface and widen our discourse possibilities. Statements by Lindof and Taylor, such as, "Ethnography of communication conceptualizes communication as a continuous flow of information, rather than as a segmented exchange of messages" (p. 44), reflect a methodological framework with roots in the early twentieth century.

Educational researchers could benefit from attending to Gadamer's (1975) argument that every concept has a history. What is today postmodern critical theory builds on theory and practice of the past and tracing and reflecting on it reinforces the claim that the history of ideas is an on-going process. It also implies that it is important to uncover the presuppositions that underlie each theoretical strand and trace the development of the ones that replace them.

We Think

My position is that what we choose to attend to and to research is not a segmented series of events but an historical and philosophical process in which implicit ideas seek to become explicit. I take this to be an absolute presupposition of Western thought. Following this, we can understand why Philipsen (1975) refers to "speech communities" and I refer to "cultural narratives."

Both of us view discourse communities as having distinct codes and norms. Philipsen wrote that "each community has its own cultural values about speaking and these are linked to judgments of situated appropriateness" (p. 13). I stress the significance of place in the creation of discourse communities and tie meaning to the development of ideas and history in a reflective, non-dialectical, non-linear and on-going process. I also argue that discourse is wider than the verbal. Gestures, music, dress, and tattoos are some examples of ways to read the world as well. I hasten to add that I am not implying that this is a theoretical suggestion that works in all cases. It's just one lens, but it is part of the picture.

Interconnectedness

Postman (2009) wrote that, "Perhaps the most important contribution schools can make to the education of our youth is to give them a sense of coherence in their studies, a sense of purpose, meaning, and interconnectedness in what they learn" (p. B12). There are several ways of thinking about this. One way is to prescribe a reading list, a grand narrative, which would lay out the expert opinions. There is a lot of merit to this approach, but problems with it as well. Another approach could be to study an edited anthology, a selected group of readings consisting of selections from great works. Once again, this is not without merit. A third way could be to divide up the topic or area into historical periods and let students self-select.

In each case a sense of coherence, purpose, meaning, and interconnectedness can be achieved but the question of the intention of the course designer and the teacher are left hanging. The selection of what is to be read entails values, and in schooling, I argue, this needs to be transparent. The way that I suggest we fulfill Postman's call is to first deconstruct the divide between teaching and learning. I have stated that both are distinct but not separate.

Teaching entails the transmission of knowledge and learning reception, however the process is a matter of thinking in circles. As we teach we should learn. As students learn they can become teachers to their peers and instructors to their teachers by reflecting and asking questions that are situated in time and place. In this way, each topic introduced becomes an excavation site and the questions the artifacts. As the process continues the site burrows further in depth of thinking skills and in relating critically to personal experience.

This is the process of fusing teaching and learning and one has the opportunity to choose any of the three alternatives listed above or more because once the teacher has declared this a process a voyage of discovery, all choice is a matter of negotiation. This is where the web becomes a vibrant source. It's not just Google. It's also the way that Wikipedia is continually constructed and deconstructed.

As teacher and learner engage in this interrelated web of process, learning becomes meaningful because it engages. It is no longer abstract because at the heart of all of this is the crafting of and relating of the small stories that define us at that moment. Further, seeing this as a process of conditionality, of as-ifing, renders us all mavericks, taking us a step outside our shells and opening up possibilities to be discussed.

Cautionary Tales, Continued

Mr. Sloan was my grade eleven history teacher, second time around. After my first dismal attempt at grade eleven, he pulled me aside and suggested that I enlist in the Army militia. This was a summer job that held out the possibility of university scholarships in fields like engineering. Although I wasn't interested in that I didn't have much else to do, so I applied and was accepted.

What I learned that summer was discipline and self-control and when I re-entered school in the fall I was better prepared. Mr. Sloan coached me through, questioning me closely when I made an assertion, suggesting alternative explanations and sources. As I look back now, I realize that he dissolved the barrier between teaching and learning.

What he did not do, however, was erase the distinction between teacher and learner. I discovered that he knew a great deal and that he was willing to share his knowledge with me in a way that applauded my probing and also my mis-takes. In that year I learned to take risks and also to recognize that my uniqueness, my divergent mind, was not necessarily a hindrance. One remarkable thing about reflection is that it often takes time to gain understanding, and in my case it took the majority of my formal education.

Link to the Past

I spent a year in the 1960s living on the Canadian prairies with my grandfather. I did this in an effort to connect to my genealogy as best I could. Granddad was my only living relative. He had immigrated to Canada the same year that the Titanic sunk, and in fact he and his new wife missed the boat and sailed the next week on their way to Australia. They never made it to Australia. My grandmother died unexpectedly and Joe, my grandfather, remained in Regina Saskatchewan.

During that year, I spent hours every day with Joe. I discovered he was born into a family of eight children in Cardiff Wales. His father was a ship carpenter who sailed the world. Joe was a master carpenter as well, and according to him, he helped build the first airplane that flew in Britain. As for me, I have trouble hammering a nail.

My grandfather sang with the prestigious Welsh Men's Choir, was the British Commonwealth senior lawn bowling champion many years running, smoked half a cigarette a day, and drank a half a bottle of beer. He was also a life member in the Masonic Lodge. One story I remember him telling me vividly was how he tried in vain to talk my father out of show business and into university. He hoped that I wouldn't make the same mis-take and he believed that I was best suited for a career in law. It meant a great deal to me that he expressed faith in me, something that I don't recall my parents doing. Previously knowing only a fraction of my heritage, I realized through my time with him that there was talent, purpose, and passion that I could try to emulate.

The Canadian prairies are a wonderfully crazy place. The winters are long and the temperatures can dip to negative 35 with wind chills making it nearly impossible to venture outside. In the short summer mosquitoes ply the skies like an invading air force, but despite the harshness there is beauty and wonder to be found and for me it was exhilarating.

In that year I double majored in History and English. I took two senior level undergraduate courses along with two of the sons of one of Canada's most celebrated novelists. What I learned in those classes I got from them as they poured out a narrative of the nature and scope of twentieth century literature as they had heard it at home. The fact that I achieved Bs in those classes was a miracle.

I also took a course in World History taught by Dr. Zarachuk, if I remember his name correctly. The course was memorable to me for several reasons; perhaps the most important was that my two English courses had primed me with ideas and creative energy. By the time I showed up in Zarachuk's class I was firing on all cylinders, as-if I was an A student. I read for meaning and discovered that with confidence I was able to remember, analyze, and synthesize. These were full year courses and each term I wrote three or four lengthy papers simultaneously. As I revised them my confidence grew and each success fueled the next. I became a writer. For once I looked forward to the final exam in World History and I was able to guess the questions and to recite quotations in my responses. Three hours later I wrote the best exam answers in my life and received a perfect score.

Finding Meaning

That spring I left my grandfather to return east to finish my degree. I left knowing more about myself from being near him and the open prairies filled with golden wheat at harvest time. I was a richer person in many ways and determined to pursue a career in academics as an historian. I believe that we find meaning in our lives through the ways that we construct our narratives about self-worth, and as we construct and reconstruct our cautionary paths we do so as a series of as-ifing possibilities.

It's ongoing, circling, reflective, and never ending. To see it as a linear map is to underestimate our potential. It's the maverick nature in us all that opens this up and teaching/learning needs to imbed this as one of its absolute presuppositions. It's who we are and who we may become.

Think of yourself as the director of a film. Sarris (1968) believed that while the actor can translate a script it is the director who speaks through the film giving it coherence and rendering it art. Your creativity can shape your life; become that work of art.

SURF'S UP

Surfing is a way of slowing down and processing stuff without consciously addressing it. A lot of the time we're forced to live in the future or the past. Surfing is something that keeps you in the present tense. Some of that is just the immediacy of the problems it sets you, physical adjustments you make every half second to stay on your feet or avoid physical injury (or discomfort, at least). Some of it is just the energy required that dulls much of your other problems. For me surfing is about beauty and connectedness. Riding a wave to shore is a lovely, meditative thing to be able to do. You're walking on water, tapping the sea's energy without extracting anything from it. You're meeting the sea, not ripping anything out of it.

—Tim Winton

As far as my father was concerned, the two years I spent in the South Pacific were a waste of my time, but for me they were liberating. In the end, what I learned from high school was that success was attainable if I followed the road map. I still didn't read or write well but my memory was excellent, so instead of reading for comprehension I memorized and then rehearsed the script I devised late at night. One thing I had in my favor was that I was able to predict fairly accurately where the teacher was headed based on previous classes. My intuition was and is pretty good. It's a tool I use.

The waves and waters of the South Pacific connected with me. It was where I was first able to truly reflect. It may seem an odd thing to say when one is riding a steep wave, but for me the pure aesthetic joy of surfing was like playing jazz. Tim Winton (2008) captured this for me in *Breath*, and although my surfing days are long gone I still hang on, by my toes, to that long board every time I write.

Being Digital: A Metaphor for our Time

You might mistakenly think of the world around us and the laws that describe it as stable and you are forgiven for that. In the late nineteenth century virtually every physicists did too. However, before the midpoint of the twentieth century, things changed completely. The electron, atomic nuclei, radioactivity, quantum theory, and the theory of relativity were either discovered or proposed during this time. Two British scientists, Michelson and Morley (1887) wrote that they had observed that the speed of light was a constant, seemingly confirming Einstein's special theory of relativity. Since that decade it has been assumed by many that the universe was unfolding as predicted.

This is a metaphor for us. On September 23rd of this year, 2011, scientists at the Large Hedron Collider at CERN observed that neutrinos apparently traveled faster than the speed of light. This cast doubt on Einstein's theory and gave substance to String Theory, which suggests 11 dimensions. By the time this book is in print this may have been settled and Einstein's work may still be correct, but two things need to be noted. First, the laws of science can never be taken as eternally true, as they are often taught in school. Second, String Theory is the first theory, to my knowledge, not based on confirmed observation. In other words, it is purely speculative, another idea that we usually don't mention in schools.

My point is that physicists realize that their field is fluid. It is never closed. This is also true, I argue, of the epistemological basis of teaching and learning and perhaps it is the absolute presupposition of the Western mind. The web and Google are making this more and more apparent to our students, but we need to make this explicit. Being digital isn't a description; it's a state of mind.

Let's swim out to the deep waters together, watch the waves come in, see which direction they are headed and which we might catch. The existence of Google, Wikipedia, and other online libraries means that rote memorization is no longer a necessary part of education. Teachers are no longer the fountain of knowledge, the internet is. Tapscott and many others since *Growing up Digital* (1998) have made this claim. To me, it's all surfing.

> On the average, we get about two percent efficiency out of school books as they are written today. The education of the future, as I see it, will be conducted through the medium of the motion picture ... where it should be possible to obtain one hundred percent efficiency.
>
> (Thomas Edison, 1922, cited in Cuban, 1986)

Steep Waves

When I first used a word processor in the mid 1980s my life changed. I had handwritten and hunt-and-peck typed my master's thesis. Typing didn't work for me. I seem to have difficulty understanding the logic of the keyboard and consequently I was slowed to a crawl with typos. Mistakes were not mis-takes with that technology.

When I was living at home in my undergraduate years my father typed my papers for me, but as a graduate student I was on my own. The consequence was that I lost confidence in myself, but halfway through my program a teacher friend introduced me to his word processor and I was surfing that steep wave again. Spelling and grammar checks were my safety nets, and as soon as I obtained my first university position I bought an Apple desktop computer. That year I wrote three articles; all of which were immediately accepted in good academic journals. I've never fallen off that wave. Stephen Hawking is right. You should concentrate on things your disability doesn't prevent you from doing well.

To Memorize or not to Memorize, is that the Question?

Is memorization a waste of time? Not for me. It is a fact that as information increases at incomprehensible speeds we all have to reinvent our knowledge bases. But I don't see this as precluding "knowing that" in the sense of memorizing, and here's why. The act of discovering where to access information is different from the act of "knowing what" information to access. This calls for critical thinking skills and the ability to conceive of the interaction of ideas over time. This is thinking historically, as Collingwood might have described it. I interact with information and call what I find "facts" if they fit my hypothesis. This is how historians work and think, but I am not claiming that these so-called facts equate to the way many scientists use the term. Historians realize that the past, as it is recovered, is fragmented.

We might think we can be certain of much of the past but uncovering why people acted as they did requires us to re-think the past. That entails understanding how we act in the present. In the end, our understanding is not an explanation but a series of judgments made by analogy. To begin this process I need to know how my mind works through reflection and how others' minds worked in the past. I have to scaffold this knowledge critically, evaluating it in the context of past paradigms and theories. It's in this step that the ability to call up reflected theories and the facts that they are embedded in can provide the springboard for my mind to make creative leaps. This partially describes how our learners construct understanding on the web.

Diverging from the Norm

I don't fit any pattern for a particular learning disability as far as I know, but then learning disabilities weren't available conditions when I was in primary school. Thinking back, it is clear I was a maverick, a divergent thinker. I had an idea about the way the universe was supposed to unfold and until shown otherwise I was going to stick to it.

The crucial point here is the primacy of narrative, both internal and external, as played out in its many forms. Bruner (1986) in his analysis of this kind of thinking examined the form of thought that goes into constructing stories or narratives. He draws an important distinction between what he calls narrative and paradigmatic modes of thinking. He stated, "The imaginative application of the paradigmatic mode leads to good theory, tight analysis, logical proof, and empirical discovery guided by reasoned hypothesis" (p. 98). This contrast is to narrative modes of thinking that lead to good stories, gripping drama, and believable historical accounts. It deals with human intention, action, and the vicissitudes and consequences that mark their course. Being a maverick or divergent thinker, is in itself an important and often neglected aspect of pedagogical praxis.

I want to use "maverick" as a concept to illustrate how thinking creatively through narratives and stories is pre-suppositional to the deconstruction of the concepts of teaching and learning. I want to stress that narratives and stories are displayed in multi-literacies and they may be explicitly stated, inferred through metaphor, or even implicitly implied through dress or gesture. In each case, though they may be distinct but they are not separate.

My evidence for this rests in the descriptions in the stories collected in the *School Stories Project* (2000) which I have been working for the past several years. These cautionary tales speak in multiple ways to the narrative of indifference to school—if not to outright scorn for the system's inability to capture and hold the imagination and the natural curiosity of children with different skill sets. It is that imaginative part of the child that is unable to concentrate and prefers to creatively wander. In many ways it is the best of the American spirit of individual creative energy that inspired Edison and others to wander into terra incognita, whether that territory is physical or mental.

The mavericks in the *School Stories* employ differing textualities and discourses as they reflect on their past educational experiences in an effort to discover or create a safe harbor, a concept borrowed from Carlson's (2002) book, *Leaving Safe Harbors*. Mavericks often don't have access to safe harbors because of social pressures, but in our fragmented and decentered world this actually benefits mavericks. They recognize and inhabit the epistemological gaps that fit their talents. I would argue that in periods of rapid change like the one in which we live, it is in the cautionary tales of mavericks that the possibilities for real change exist.

These tales make explicit the epistemological gaps and suggest that we think of the world as a series of as-ifing opportunities. This is an important point because if we can fuse teaching and learning as I am suggesting, formal education becomes an ongoing process, where evaluation is cumulative and where theory and practice ultimately collapse into a form of social praxis that is essentially and basically democratic.

For mavericks, creativity is multi-dimensional, experiential, and we often see signs of it in intellects with diverse experiences and perspectives. Florida (2002) suggested that diversity, openness, and acceptance of difference are crucial elements in the development of a creative class of mavericks (p. 294). I would add that formal education plays a large part in this equation. When schools are open and accepting of difference in teaching and learning, good things can happen.

A fact that is worth thinking about, and one that Florida often mentions, is that little or no attention is paid to this. I have said that my references to mavericks are not to individuals but to the concept of "maverickness." My point is that we can make a place for divergent thoughts and actions in the classroom and in society if for no other reason than they illustrate how important divergent thinking is to help us shift the epistemological strands. Often it is mavericks who lead us into new ages. In spite of this, we make scant use of their talents inside and outside of our schools. In the context of this book, most of the thinkers I refer to exhibit maverick traits. It is also striking how these people are able to collapse categories and how this ability could be used in a positive way in our schools.

I'm on that 30 Foot Wave!

My framework here is intellectual and academic but it is driven by my personal experiences. While many of our day-to-day decisions are not in this category, some of them are. Therefore, while it is true that information is coming in at lightning speed, knowing that continues to remain a necessary but not sufficient condition for being able to teach and learn. In iBrain: Surviving the Technological Alteration of the Modern Mind, Small and Vorgan (2009) stated that our exposure to the net is impacting the way our brains form neural pathways. Wiring up our brains like this makes us adept at filtering information and making snap decisions. Being able to see the bigger picture, synthesizing, and reading the multiple discourses that comprise our cultural narrations should be thought of as precluding the other. As this century blossoms my guess is that mavericks will be successful at both levels. I don't think they will have any choice.

My generation grew up having to memorize historical dates and mathematical formulas, and for me that was very difficult, but at the same time freeing as it allowed me time for ideas to "sink in." These so-called facts were a clothes hanger. I now see this as reflexion and it has been essential for me.

These days, if I need to know the exact year something happened or a person's name I know that Google is there and that Wikipedia can point me quickly in the direction I need to go, but that direction is in the process of being determined. It's not a road map. It is as-ifed by me, one wave at a time, every step of the way from a general, but informed, idea to a well thought out opinion. I realize that many students continuously multi-task. They text and surf the net while listening to music and updating their Facebook page, but learning isn't an either/or proposition.

Up on the Curl

Tapscott, Robinson, Pink, Leadbeater, and others are all correct to tell us that education needs to change. But paradigms don't change in a flash, as Kuhn wrote. Yes, the time of the "sage on the stage" is outdated, but it is still common practice and is likely to remain so for the foreseeable future. I want us to move to a model where purpose, mastery, autonomy, and reflection are presuppositions of a fused teaching and learning, where the process is negotiated and often linear, but still values the transmission of direct knowledge.

Plato and Socrates are still in the building. They initiated interactive education and though this is a different time, we need to recognize the power and meaning of past thoughts. That's the secret to it all. Think historically about what happened and why, how it fits, and why eventually it didn't. Think dialectically and then factor in your personal self and your ability to quick source. Now it's a trialectic. We're still up on that curl.

I often get quickly unraveled when asked to recite facts. My mind wanders and my curiosity allows me to go places in my imagination that others don't. However, realizing that I make these connections also allows me to know them by heart, I just don't use a linear path and consequently my take is different from Tapscott's views. Where he perceives the old school model as a waste of time, I sense an opportunity for deconstruction, reconstruction, negotiation, and collaboration.

Pipeline

Given the interactive nature of our lives in the digital age, we have the tools to harness different forms of attention and take advantage of them. In part, this book proposes a different way of seeing. One that's based on multi-tasking our information and considering ideas from sources we might not have considered. This is what the web can offer us. Davidson (2011) said, "Multitasking is the ideal mode of the 21st century, not just because of information overload but also because our digital age was structured without anything like a central node broadcasting one stream of information that we pay attention to at a given moment.

On the Internet, everything links to everything, and all of it is available all the time. Davidson makes his point by saying that research indicates that, at every age level, people take their writing more seriously when it will be evaluated by peers than when it is to be judged by teachers. Online blogs written for students' peers exhibit fewer typographical and factual errors, less plagiarism, and generally better, more elegant and persuasive prose than classroom assignments by the same writers.

I often have a difficult time convincing my students that quality is more important than quantity. Although surveys show that the amount of time our children spend on homework has risen over the past three decades, American students are mired in the middle of international academic ratings. It's not a matter of a new fix or a new set of tires, we need to understand that the generation of students who has grown up on the web and who now are entering higher education approach schooling in a very different way than the people who designed it or the people who run it.

This emerging generation realizes that much of the work that needs to be done doesn't require close reading of text. When a problem or task is assigned, the smart learner discovers where that exact information is and accesses it. What they don't do is read an entire book, chapter, or article in the process. They chunk, surf, discuss, and collaborate in a non-linear fashion where what needs to be done is often a negotiated group effort. After all, isn't this the way that your day works? This isn't to say that students don't read entire books. Reading for pleasure or passion is a different kind of reading and they know it.

Since we cannot know what knowledge will be needed in the future it is senseless to try to teach it in advance. Instead our job must be to try to turn out young people who love learning so much, and who learn so well, that they will be able to learn whatever needs to be learnt.

—Holt, 1964

A Beginning

The obvious question is, "How then can you teach and learn in our schools?" My answer is to ask different questions, "why" questions. I begin by grounding students' interest in the topic we are studying in their own experience. We begin on a vast ocean and bit by bit we become more explicit and specific, always reflecting about the ideas read about and our negotiated and shared responses. I'm integral to that process because I require my students to submit draft after draft of their work until their voices are authentic and their opinions sound. I'm trying to make them feel prepared for the unfolding world that awaits them, not with a map but with a Wikipedia mindset.

So, what will learners need to be successful in a workplace where the jobs they may get have yet to be created? They will need people skills for this diverse world, collaborative skills, and higher order thinking skills. Students will have need of the ability to analyze and synthesize, as well as autonomy. Mostly, they need to believe that a blend of formal and informal education will help them in this. Right now it often doesn't.

So Last Century

For more than a hundred years schools have indoctrinated learners into believing that the world of work was arranged in a hierarchical order. Schools defined knowledge in terms of specialization while the world slowly morphed. Today, information and knowledge don't move in a linear manner. Seldom is anyone really "in charge" any more. More commonly, information is sent out, distributed on the web, interpreted by various people, then through negotiation its meaning is constructed.

Our world of information is a continual pipeline. It's true that we aren't machines. We are complex and ambiguous while we strive for coherence. So, while the web beckons us to cooperate and share, we shouldn't be surprised when we want to be alone to think, write, and react. The dialectical model just doesn't fit in today's world. It's isn't matter of an either/or thesis and anti-thesis and resolutions are seldom if ever straight forward. The web deconstructs and simultaneously reconstructs. It's in a state of flux, constantly emerging, and we give it shape and meaning in part on what we have learned culturally and in part from direct experience. There's no formula. Teaching and learning, memorizing and reacting, are all members of the same category.

Borderlands

Today, our epistemological borderlands are not as opaque and ideas of difference are often nudged unacknowledged. So, what are we to do? Many of our students believe that cultural and historical presuppositions that they memorize do not reflect the way that they make meaning. Today's learners do not limit belief and understanding to just what is spoken and written. It was previously assumed that language, spoken and written, was the gauge for us to communicate, but that is no longer the case. Language is simply one of many possible multimodalities, though it is a historically privileged one. As we move into a period of fluidity and apparent chaos, things appear to fall apart. This is because we cling to spoken and written language as the absolute basis for our understanding.

For many learners, language is just one of many possibilities. Students construct and deconstruct in a multitude of ways on an as-needed, just-in-time basis. This is a different kind of discourse than we have developed in so-called modern society, but it does have echoes to the middle ages and the emergence of print. Today, learners rely on their electronic devices for information; information that teachers and schools provided in the past. They see the world as one where there are multiple possibilities, multiple ways of knowing, and a world where there is more than one map to get us from point A to point B.

As teachers, we need to make explicit the cultural and historical modes of communication that we use in our classroom discourse. Doing this is a first step, as it acknowledges a world of multiplicity and it allows us to negotiate a semiotic understanding based in a multimodal belief of the historical construction and understanding of everyday discourse. We can interact in virtual worlds as well as print worlds. New technologies can enhance communication, but no technology can erase the historical presuppositions of a culture.

Discourse, like text, can be any perceived object. Students know well that just because something can't be put into ordinary language, that doesn't mean it does not exist or cannot be understood. So much of street discourse and the unacknowledged discourses of the classroom are located in these borderlands. They often aren't spoken but displayed as graffiti, dance, or body art. These intermodal images communicate in a way that is not simply neglected in the schools but is also ignored and discounted by the caretakers of the standards.

Establishing standards for the English language and its usage has always been a matter of negotiation not legislation, always that is, except in school. Somehow, despite all the research to the contrary, we have it in our heads that school-age children don't have the ability to move beyond the dominant discourse and that it is our role to police this cognitive process. Anyone who holds this view really ought to get out more and listen to the many creative ways in which discourse is being constructed and language games are being played.

Symbolism, representations, language, and the like do not transcend their meaning in the material world when relocated into virtual worlds. Humans interact in both worlds, so the cultural and historical modes of communication we use every day are still present as we interact in virtual worlds. Multimedia does have the ability to enhance communication, but it cannot rid language of cultural implications and historical symbolism. All of this is currently the case and it also affects the way that we make sense of the past.

Schama (1995) and Collingwood (1946) make the point that history is written by historians selecting particular actions as facts. I would push this further. The discourses that historians have acknowledged have been of a certain kind and, since the birth of writing and then publishing, these discourses have been largely linear and print text. In the past thirty years, historians have discovered that other stories in other discourse forms are also available. Autobiographies, fables, dances, and songs all qualify as good historical data. They also count as forms of discourse that I need to acknowledge and attend to in my teaching and learning.

Categorization is not limited to history either. We apply the same linearality to our educational discourse. For many of us, meaning has to have a direct connection to what is perceived and therefore taken to be the case. As a student of history I became aware of the many ways that meaning is transferred in a culture and over time. For example, the birth of European National Socialism in the early twentieth century was based on the explicit establishment of a set of presuppositions about what is true, beautiful, and correct.

While World War II brought an end to this political mindset, it did not impact the lives of many other people. Most citizens in Western society remained convinced that a grand narrative or a set of grand narratives existed which defined the limits and forms of knowledge. The intellectual history of the twentieth century proved that not to be true. As we rush into the twenty-first century, it is becoming more evident that there has been a crack in our cosmic egg.

In fact, it's more like Humpty Dumpty. We can't put it back together again. This isn't something to grieve over. Many groups, such as women, people of color, children, and those holding diverse views on many topics have been left out of the conversation and declared "others." In the last one hundred years we have witnessed the slow fusing of peoples.

As structures fall apart under the demand for transparency, new forms of discourse arise and the form and nature of reading and writing as well as teaching and learning changes with them. Physics through Heisenberg, history and philosophy through Collingwood and Wittgenstein, anthropology through Douglas illuminated multiple ways of knowing and defining a field of study. This epistemological shift became explicit because of the multimodal nature of new technology. The boundary between teacher and learner became blurred. The ownership of knowledge was likewise up for discussion as it became possible to write and re-write an encyclopedia online. Expertise is no longer tied to race, color, gender, or a university degree.

Leaving Safe Harbor

The thought flashed through my mind as the wave broke and I was free. The ship was huge. Although I had traveled across the continent, I wasn't ready for what came next. I had stood in a line where more than a thousand of us curled like ants towards the quay, weaving our way through a vast terminal in the early morning. With my documents, passport, and boarding pass in my hand I made my way up to the platform that took me to another world.

I stepped aboard and was given general directions on how to find my room, located beneath the surface with no porthole. I shared my room with three others and we didn't part company until three weeks later in Auckland, New Zealand. I discovered a great deal about life that I could not have imagined, but that day as we cast away from the port of Vancouver I realized that I was leaving all that I knew, all that was familiar to me. I had craved this opportunity and now it was mine. It was the opportunity to re-invent myself. The blue of the Pacific, the white of the liner's wake, and the endless horizons blended into something mystical. I had left my safe harbor believing that anything was possible. The past was done and the future uncharted. What I came to realize was that the past is always there in various forms, the task is to make it meaningful. Our possibilities are shaped by this.

Surfing with William Gibson: A Temporality

The theory of Atemporality is based on the fact that with clocks one measures duration, speed, and numerical order of material change, not time. With one's eyes, one can perceive in the universe only material changes that run into physical space. One cannot perceive time as a physical reality into which material changes run. Material change runs into physical space only and not in time. Time is not a fundamental physical reality as matter, energy, and physical space are. Time exists only when we measure it; time is an "observer effect."

The Universe is an atemporal phenomenon and that time exists into man, not the other way around. Time itself cannot be observed in the universe. There is no past and no future. Atemporality is also used to describe much of the current music scene which appears to fade from newness to newness. Gibson (2010) used atemporality to refer to the absence of contemporaneity. It appears that the web has allowed us to bypass time via YouTube, Netflix, and iTunes. This allows us to not only re-visit but to re-enact cultural actions as-if they were occurring now.

What is going on? Well, for one thing, you are showing your age. This isn't half as confusing to learners in our classrooms. At least that's my experience. That's what they tell me. They have grown up experiencing a world where concepts are in the process of emerging. They learn when they need to or want to and what they learn is mostly directed at answering or solving an immediate problem or concern. They don't "read" as we were taught but they are "surf literate."

What appears strange to them is the idea that truths are fixed and eternal and that knowledge could be coded into one grand narrative. What is important and pre-suppositional is sharing and community. Learning is cooperative, yet learning communities are always in flux and interactive. It is relative to place but not necessarily to time as it has been measured in modern capitalistic society and that is the framing of educational practice. Greenblatt (2011) would say we've taken a "swerve."

Let's Swerve Again

When Schmidt gave the 2011 MacTaggart lecture, he began by saying that the web is less than 30 years old and that it is hard to imagine life without it. This is how the Luddites felt in the eighteenth century when England began to industrialize and household arts and crafts began to be pushed aside. Modernization meant that all of a sudden nothing seemed secure. Every person's identity, everything that seemed known was thrown into doubt.

That is the same effect the web has had and we are slowly coming to understand that the changes are more far-reaching than we could ever have imagined. It's not just that we can access information more quickly. It's the fact that we can access anything and construct our personal meaning without consulting experts. We self-diagnose our illnesses, redefine democracy to justify our beliefs, and critique any idea or any person armed with whatever source we choose to call on. This type of relativism is new and it can be dangerous. It can lead to dogmatism and tyranny, so we better discover quickly how to incorporate the web into our social fabric.

Right now, computers can recognize facial features and gestures, can cope with complex grammatical questions, and can navigate cars safely on the road to avoid accidents. These features are wonderful, but in this world of complexity and community can we safely share, protect privacy, and empower people without anarchy? How do we craft a passage to the future where the "fortunate few" work with the "less fortunate many" and not against them?

The same questions were asked in eighteenth century England. Their answer was an on-going dialectical conversation upon which our modern democracy was forged. It's been a bumpy road, paved with many good intentions but also with greed and self-interest. In today's world of open access, we need a reformulation and this is occurring through interactivity.

Social networking allows us almost real time as well as head time. We can almost be inside peoples' heads and almost understand what they say and think. Believing this to be true is a heavy burden for both teachers and learners. As we surf our minds via the web, we collect bites and artifacts. We must remember to reflect on the good reasons to believe these opinions, as well as to make explicit our understanding of them, and be willing to negotiate their personal and collective worth. Knowing has become fluid, open-ended and nonlinear. It's about now, but it's also about then and why, and about me and us.

In the eighteenth and nineteenth centuries, the British established and maintained an educational system where science and the arts were both integral to becoming well-educated. Lewis Carroll who wrote *Alice in Wonderland* was also a mathematician. Einstein was both a physicist and a poet. Tolkien was a master storyteller and linguist. T. S. Elliot was an accomplished poet and philosopher. All of these great thinkers combined natural and physical sciences with some form of artistic expertise.

Today, we are pushing students to become experts in narrowly defined fields. It has become an either/or world, but the web encourages us to pursue what makes us happy, not just what gets us a job. It also encourages us to do things without compensation, in cooperation with others. There's something happening here and it is very clear (my apologies to the Buffalo Springfield) that teachers and learners are rediscovering a passion for broad-based learning. Ken Robinson (2011) put this argument so well that millions have watched his TedTalk, and in the process they are changing education in a way unthinkable to politicians.

I can access my passion at a time that suits me, anywhere I wish. I can repeat, pause, or fast forward. In short, it is possible for me to learn what I want when and where I want, and as I do so I become the person I wish to be. As teachers, we need to provide these opportunities and to support them. As learners, we need to leave our save harbor and seek these opportunities in a way that invites our teachers to share in the process. Teachers have a lot of deep knowledge and personal experiences to share. Together, teachers and learners can negotiate, deconstruct, and reconstruct. Together, we can construct a new paradigm.

Fluidity and discontinuity are central to the reality in which we live.

—Mary Catherine Bateson

Fluidity

Anyone who has surfed on a board or with his body knows about the fluidity of water. It's constantly moving, shifting patterns and colors. In every way one can imagine, it feels alive. Being on the water in a ship makes you even more aware of this. The motion of a vessel as it carves it way across an ocean is something magical and mystical. There can be days and even weeks when the sea is placid, and then out of nowhere things shift and the ocean becomes a beast. In education, we have tended to ignore discontinuity and fluidity in favor of what can is predicted. That has come to be regarded as the nature of things. In fact, the last one hundred years have shown us that much of our thinking emanates in serendipity. It is nonlinear and sometimes circular. Currently, this is described as being complex and chaotic, and it may well be in comparison to a world that can be mapped, charted, and predicted.

Public education in the Western world has presupposed that the world is orderly and can be described and taught in this way. It has worked in the sense that a logical positivist perspective has fit our economic and social patterns and it has served as a blueprint as well in its expression as a grand narrative.

The trouble is that a lot of the time our world is messy, fragmented, and decentered. As we rediscover the power of storytelling and autobiography, we also deconstruct large narratives and reconstruct personal stories as cautionary tales, tales that are relative to place and person. Tim Beresford Lee, who discovered the web, had no idea that his work would change the epistemological landscape as it has. Google, Wikipedia, Linux, Twitter, and Apple have each in their own way rendered understanding and knowledge as a shared community project. Each questions concepts such as ownership, sharing, community, and creativity as well as the nature and definition of knowledge.

This is a paradigm shift and it means that in order to thrive in this new set of shifting presuppositions we have to understand and integrate all facets of life. We also have to get better at a lot of things in regards to teaching and learning.

Riptide

Anyone who lives near the ocean is familiar with a riptide. In places where waves are consistently strong there is an on-going pattern of wave formations, cresting and then the denouement of crashing on the shore. People who live in and by the sea as surfers are also intimately acquainted with the force of the sea returning to its depths to begin again. This circularity is also found in human expression, as Douglas has chronicled. The myths of ancient Greece and Rome were circular, as were medieval plays, circling back to every man and his quest for salvation.

In fact, much of what we call great art in Western civilization follows this pattern. I raise these points to draw your attention again to my plea to reexamine the dialectic. Modernism plotted a path of narrowly defined consistent progress, often disregarding ethical and moral presuppositions that have given us metaphysical and epistemological roots. A new paradigm beckons and my guess is that it will have floating presuppositions, relative to place and time. In this paradigm, truth will be a matter of specificity, not generality, and broad human input will be foundational, not extraordinary.

I argue for this path because of the enduring importance of human expression. Whether it is oral or written, chanted or scripted, danced or sketched on canvas, on the computer or on our bodies, an intrinsic element of being human is our desire to make what I shall call "music." Music is circular, bending and folding back on itself in constant and continual reflexion.

It is in this spirit that I approach the introduction of the vast array of new technologies and their impact. Instead of an either/or epistemology, let me suggest an on-going process of offering as-ifing presuppositions, each with the specific purpose of asking a specific question within the historical context of previous presuppositions. Each presupposition emanates from inside our heads. Each presupposition is a fact based on the best evidence available, but each is also contingent upon the possibility of new archeological digs and artifacts. In other words, each presupposition is a conditional as-ifing.

Take, for instance, this statement: The internet is making the world more open, fairer, and more prosperous. If thought of as a truth claim in ordinary language, then it is predictive and either true or false. But if taken as a conditional statement, it appears as-if the internet may enable us to be more open, fairer, and prosperous then it is not a claim, but a relative comment on our current state of affairs.

The difference between these two is not unimportant. In fact, it is only significant because it frames discourse as being invitational, personal, and historical as well as negotiable. My claim is based on the assumptions that discourse, in its multiplicity, is a process in which we are predisposed to make what it implicit explicit. As Collingwood may have put this, we reason for what we think to be the case is because of what we choose to think of as evidence. If I know how my mind works then, by analogy, I can think through the reasons why someone acted as they did. Therefore, all knowledge is self-knowledge.

PRACTICAL APPLICATIONS TO PEDAGOGY

Pass the Popcorn

"Be quiet," I say to myself as the person next to me wolfs down another handful of popcorn and then gulps what sounds like a gallon of soda. I'm trying to concentrate on the movie. On the screen, Vito Mortgenson is standing in front of a gang describing and explaining who he is. *Eastern Promises* is one of the movies that impacted me in a dramatic way in the past few years. It is an example of just how much our conception of language and discourse has changed. In the scene I am referring to, Mortgenson takes off his shirt and reads the tattoos on his body to his audience, a group of gangsters. Each tattoo is a cautionary tale and each tells more about him than any written description ever could to this audience. Each member of his audience is familiar with the discourse, knows how to read it, and accepts its authenticity. The meaning of the narrative, however, is discussed and negotiated.

I can envision something similar to this happening every day, but where the form of discourse is different. It might be in a formal job interview where the candidates resume is discussed. It could be a performance on a stage or an athlete demonstrating her skills in front of coaches. Lastly, we could locate something like this in a classroom, when the language game of question and answer is at play. To understand how there are multiple possibilities, we need to "see" the world as sets of complex and loosely interwoven actions, each tied through negotiated decoding in ways that are increasing with every new version of Google, Twittier, or new iPad. It's fair to say that in some ways technology now drives epistemology. What we want to do is link them, and that is the object of this chapter.

To construct meaning from our shifting strands one has to recognize the diversity of discourse possibilities, and to be able to enter into a negotiated dialogue about the meaning. In part this is the theme of this chapter, but it's wider and deeper than tattoos. Gesture, art, music, and dress have become dominate signifiers, giving name and meaning and they are displacing more traditional textualities, like written text. In the following pages, I invite you to consider the strands that I continue to describe as a series of shifting threads. Each may be necessary for any one of us to construct meaning, but for common discourse and cultural understanding it is becoming clear that no one thread is by itself sufficient. We weave our own melodies and we come to understand in this decentered and fragmented world by continually negotiating the key we are playing in our shifting strands.

This is one reason, and perhaps a central one, that teaching and learning are problematic in schooling as it is presently structured. I don't have tattoos, but I do have signifiers. We all do, but we may not be aware of them. Because I was a sick kid I lived on the fringes of social constructs. I was a loner by necessity and eventually by design. In my early childhood, polio was a national concern and because no one really knew what was wrong with me, I was ordered to stay away from crowds, beaches, and playgrounds. That was okay with me because I was able to discover a dog or a group of dogs to hang out with. They were and are some of my best friends.

As I grew up I came to recognize that not only dress but language could be used to signify difference. I would carefully monitor what I said and expunged any jargon that my contemporaries might have used, like "cool," to demonstrate that I was not part of any group or clique. I also made a point of wearing my hair the opposite way of the trend, short when it was fashionable for it to be long and long when it was "cool" to have it short. In high school music class, I selected the tuba not the trumpet, though I knew how to play the trumpet, like my father. That's still how I am. My signifiers are there to be read.

> Sometimes the "you" in my songs is me talking to me. Other times I can be talking to somebody else. When I say "I" right now, I don't know who I'm talking about.

> —Bob Dylan

Reading Ourselves

Let's assume for a minute that thinking about the type of ideas that we are dealing with in this book is based upon our ability to know ourselves and therefore, by analogy, others. Let us also ground that in language games and multiple forms of discourse and assume that curriculum theory is an on-going reflexive process of self-discovery and self-creation. If we can accept these premises, then curriculum might be cast as a methodology about the development of thought, a process in which all of human experience would be included. Each subject might become the discovery of the essence of mind, in which the outcome is the latest expression of our ideas about how we think. It would not be a final solution. In short, this presents us with the possibility to construct a community of diverse learners by creating, listening, and critically reflecting on our as–if stories about the world.

Importantly, the as-ifing of our narratives allows us to escape the modernist dilemma of the use of analogy to uncover meaning about the ways that others think. By as-ifing narratives we pose the possibility of constructing meaning, rather than imposing it. As-ifing the curriculum takes us further than Collingwood's (1940) theory of metaphysics allowed us to understand our world. Instead of making the assumption that the explicit presuppositions, or underlying ideas, of a time can be uncovered by rational thinking, as-ifing supposes that knowing about the world is a process of mediated construction of coming to know ourselves and our horizon.

A Circling Thread: Seminalities

In less confusing and complex times our signifiers were often prescribed for us by society. Today, we mix, blend, and construct our signifiers to match our current "self." They have become our conditionals, our as-ifs, and they shift from moment to moment. That is one of the most important aspects of this. Social media allows us to become who we wish to be, or who we see in the mirrors or Twitter or Facebook. That vision is constantly under construction. This is understood by almost every student but few teachers, and that's an epistemological divide. Multimedia, multi-representation, and multiple literacies have created what Kress (2007) called a multimodal world. Kress referred to this as the implicit symbols in language. Words have specific meaning and other factors can add multiple dimensions to language, which can then be translated into written and/or virtual texts.

We know that our students interact easily in both worlds. So, bridging this gap means to explicitly invite a conversation about meaning; one that in its own way unearths the presuppositions of all members in the conversation. This negotiation is a basic building block in decoding, but it is about more than decoding. It is about the construction of meaning through historical re-enactment and collapsing the categories of philosophical thought. So we ask the question, "What is in the mind of the person writing, displaying, or singing this?" Through this process, we deconstruct the signifiers and negotiate meaning; meaning that is both relative and true to the as-ifed presuppositions.

Keep in mind that I am referring to historical presuppositions, not absolute presuppositions. For Collingwood and other philosophers, these relative presuppositions characterized an historical epoch. Today, they frame a conversation. For me, every thing can be taken as a sign that stands for something else, namely words, images, sounds, and gestures. It may be easier to understand how semiotics relates to teaching and learning if one thinks about how an anthropologist tries to make meaning of the world that he or she happens upon. In each case, understanding is constructed by making sense of signs presented in various textual forms.

Let me illustrate. Levi-Strauss (1963) created a dialogue with his materials and illustrates how best to use them. He asked how the process of discovery leads to making meaning, and then he tracked that process. What he didn't do was lay down the path of what that meaning will be beforehand. So, semiotics calls for anthropologists, teachers, and students to construct personal meaning from actions. This is a reversal of the traditional curriculum process, and of traditional teaching and learning practices. Learning becomes a creative act shaped by the intentions of the learner and also by language, social, and psychological factors.

A Mind Walk

Gunther Kress (2007) said that multi-modality is a fact of life in all forms of public discourse and the question is just what signs and symbols we will use. This is open to negotiation at this point, and the result will be a new definition of culture. When I read Kress I feel as though I am listening to a piece of music written by Philip Glass, where each note and each instrument complement each other in distinct yet connected ways. Not only do we appear to share common threads about the nature of teaching and learning, but his writing exhilarates me. I believe that much of what he has written recently is powerful and brilliant. In this book, my aim is to weave the various strands of curriculum theory in a different way from that which is traditionally presented, and to suggest a re-boot of some of the theoretical foundation. Get ready to hit the trail with me.

It should be clear by now that my lenses are both historical and philosophical, whereas Kress comes at this from a different perspective. Nonetheless, I find significant resonances in his work that I will draw on and circle back to during the argument I am building in the book. You might say I am as-ifing, and that is my aim. A further aim is to point to the importance of a broad cross-fertilization of ideas. Educational theory is in desperate need of thinkers outside the field.

The Path Forks

We need a theory that deals with meaning in all its appearances, in all social occasions, and in all cultural sites. Kress labels that theory with the title of his 2010 book, *Social Semiotics*. In broad terms, Kress's work applies to all cultures but it is grounded in individual experience, or place, and "not universals but shared by all cultures, based on experiences in their engagement common to humans in social groups" (p. 13) in their power relationships with each other and their cultures. In such a context, language in its widest sense becomes just one means to make meaning and this also shows the boundlessness of language.

I have previously written (2007, 2008, 2009, 2010 and 2011) that our understanding of various forms of discourse needs to be broadened because of the way that we all access data or information. Our decentered and fragmented world is in the process of developing new sets of presuppositions and one of those has to do will the ease and speed with which we access information. Gesture, image, music, and dress are no longer separate and distinct. They are part of an on-going process that I characterize as the nature of mind in the Western world. What I am engaged in is an attempt to make meaning under one roof, but where meaning is not unified except in the process of its negotiation.

It is true that we are everywhere connected (Kress, 2010), but it is really more than this. Rather the driver is the way that we approach globalization again. I say again because the idea of globalization goes back at least to the Romans and our understanding of it is tied to the presuppositions of our paradigm. How we see ourselves, others, and our culture and how we employ discourses shapes this view. What is important to note is that this time our relative presuppositions about globalization are not just self-oriented. They are communal, negotiable, and in flux. In part, this is because we are truly multimodal. The dominant mode of representation is no longer writing. It is image, and that is constantly being altered. What we need is a new discourse based on generalizable, semiotic principles common to all. I refer to this as a set of relative presuppositions. I also see it as historically and philosophically driven. As Kress stated, signs form meaning and "are expressions of interest given outward expression and shaped by practices of a culture are interactive" (p. 10).

A Shifting Landscape

I now want to expand the notion of semiotics. Signs in their various forms are invitations, not flags. They don't stand alone in any general or specific sense. In each case, their meaning has to be negotiated at multiple levels and that is one clear message from social networking. Kress is right to say that there are some broad general patterns. I call these paradigms framed by relative presuppositions, but these merely frame in today's discourse world. They give a place to begin to construct common discourse that I call "Semiotics 2.0" or "polymodal."

Meanings are specific to a particular culture, yet actively chosen for an intended understanding. Meaning is constructed in a non-linear manner in an historical context that is linear, and yet personal and relative. What is becoming clear is that the process of making meaning explicit and the move from implicit to explicit is constantly "up for grabs." It's a never-ending process, where the majority of what we say we mean is cautionary, fragmented, and decentered. This doesn't toss us into a relativist hole because we construct meaning on an as-if basis. Everything is momentarily "the case." If, as in empirical fields, it can hold together over a long period of time, then it becomes a law or qualifies as a truth. But in our day-to-day world it is different. Here we are shift changing. Polymodalities are ways of expressing and displaying this. As we move from a print- based culture to one of new and expanding possibilities introduced by technology, we also move to a conditional as-if discourse of a different kind.

In this polymodal landscape, I have a number of ways of expressing and shaping my message. The questions that confront me are: Which is best for the meaning I wish to communicate? Which mode matches my interests or appeals to my intended audience? Which medium will my audience attend to? These are questions all educators need to consider. No longer is it a matter of presenting a text and then requiring learners to read a chapter and answer the questions at the back of the book. How I position myself is a factor of which medium I am operating in.

All of your responses to these questions ought to be based on your assessment of the context of your environment. This is a complex and often fast-moving set of actions interweaving, circling, and reforming as they play themselves out. This is the classroom of life. It's not linear or predictable, and certainly not chartable in terms of high stakes testing. It's evolving, and a process that is often at any instant more relative than stable. I argue that we are currently in such a world. A world of shifting strands of presuppositions which re-form in on-going motions. In such a world, we need to invite conversation and to negotiate meaning, however transitory it may be.

Yes, this is for the moment, because learning is often exactly that. Is that all there is? No, of course not, but at the present time in our classrooms, it's crucial. Everything, after all, is a message for us to interpret.

It's very complex and unstable, I argue. Our contemporary, social world is increasingly fragmented, decentered, and individualistic. In times like these, individual communication becomes problematic. Each conversation presupposes questions about social and 'political' relations, tastes, needs and desires and each needs to continually re-visited.

In this Polymodal World

For Kress (2007), the concept of multimodality alludes to the implicit symbols in language. Words have specific meaning and other factors, such as size, add multiple dimensions to language which can be translated into both written and virtual texts. We know that our students interact easily in both worlds. What is not so clear is that teachers or their curricula do. This is an epistemological gap that can be bridged. Learners and teachers can and should work collaboratively to discover how it is possible to be with others "as-if" one knows what it means to be thoughtful and tactful in this de-centered world.

Polymodalities

A close friend of mine, Tom Rose, associates making meaning with artistic metaphors. As for me, I see, hear, and think in musical metaphors. The best word that I know to begin to describe this is polyphony. This term refers to music whose texture is formed by the interweaving of several melodic lines, which are independent but blend together harmonically. Polyphony has its roots in mediaeval music, but today it is being adapted through the use of multiple musical "voices." Multi-voiced groups like The Polyphonic Spree, a choral symphonic pop rock band which utilizes a choir, flute, trumpet, trombone, violin, viola, cello, percussion, piano, guitars, bass, drums, electronic keyboards, and EWI, produce many sounds simultaneously.

Think of this in terms of modality. Here we have two or more people each constructing their own meaning in such a way that, in musical terms, each has his or her own melody. It's more than multiplicity and complexity, but also incorporating threads of chaos theory infused by the principle of self-organization. I have described this previously as part of as–ifing, but here I want to add a polymorphic process.

Understanding is based on signs, symbols, and texts and when the voices play together a process of understanding and meaning can be constructed. But like appreciating a painting or piece of music, each of us makes our own meaning. Sharing our constructions by as-ifing in a historically-based manner is the shared critical process. This is an important point for educators to contemplate because if self-understanding is based upon historical interpretation, then perhaps understanding the nature and roles of language and history are crucial for recognizing ourselves based in what Ricoeur (2005) called mutual recognition. Here is another melody to consider in our quest for a meaningful curriculum theory.

Teaching and Learning are Threaded in an As-ifing Weave

It has become explicitly obvious with each passing decade that it is the small stories of our lives that have become the only meaningful pieces on which our lives can be grounded. As learners, we know that the above description is accurate; as teachers, we realize that we must put this thought into our practice.

Gramsci (1971) called this process "praxis." His conception of the relationship between thinking (theory) and doing (practice) frees us from any urge to construct a false dichotomy as if theory and practice were separate. In fact, on this account, the two are distinct but not separate parts of our minds. It is necessary to recognize the uniqueness and singularity of our own narratives and life stories to give us personal and shared meaning. Recognizing this point allows us to play with theory "as-if" it were simply that, a theory. It may also be helpful here to think of theory as a mode of thinking about varying concepts, one of them text. Earlier, I referred to the ways in which ideas from many different fields have come together to inform us about the concept of curriculum. In the postmodern world in which we live, the small narratives of the development of ideas flow and intermingle across disciplines and national boundaries.

Tochon (2002) broadened semiotics in an interesting way that fits with my thinking. He argued that educators have constructed a culture of niceness around the act of teaching that negates the ethical nature of what happens in good classrooms with experienced and caring teachers. This culture of niceness prevents teachers and students from understanding the problems associated with teaching and learning as they try to make meaning of the world of education. In his book, *Tropics of Teaching*, Tochon described semiotics as the ethical element of teaching. It is what good, experienced teachers do when they care for their students.

They become flexible in their pedagogical practice. This ethical quality is highly prized by our society, but for the most part it has not been addressed in faculties of education or in school classrooms. The reason for the split between theory and practice, Tochon stated, is that we have forgotten that teaching is the mirror to the soul and not based upon the rational reflection of how to make things fit. We have further confused the meaning of such key concepts as word and actions, ideology and change, and economics and education. And we have lost touch with what is most important: contact. Contact occurs during a conversation between a teacher and a student when it is based upon a bottom-up discovery of the learning process. It is not a prescribed path to defined ends. Teaching is the art of translating signs from art to poetry and beyond. This world is not just found in books, computers, or audio/video. It surrounds us.

In the same way, meaning is not simply transmitted to us. We actively create it according to a complex interplay of codes, of which we are unaware. I think this point is vital. University education in particular is often accused of not preparing students for the real world. Given my description above I think we could say that too often teaching does not touch base in order for us to understand signs. In many cases, if signs are learned they are not made explicit, and therefore no real meaning is made. Too often students pick up meanings implicitly and the pedagogical moment is lost.

This process of humanist reflection enables us to understand how this differs from what we traditionally do in our schools. Tochon organized his ideas around three metaphors: "productivity" (or output and standardization), "warfare" (or strategy and expertise), and finally "priesthood" (or the enlightened subject). He argued that we can by-pass these three concepts by employing a semiotic methodology he called his counter-methodology. The counter-methodology would be learning activities based upon lived experiences as opposed to top-down plan oriented activities.

One example of this, according to Tochon, is action poetry. He believed that the city of Geneva had lost touch with its soul and this was exhibited by the lack of public interest in poetry. He took advantage of a local grant and had students write original poems about matters of personal interest to them. Each of the twenty-seven original poems was then inscribed by hand in acrylic by a professional painter and then mounted on billboards all over the city. The reaction was just what he had hoped for: a public conversation in all the media about the poems. This initiated other new and giant poems on billboards and many are still visible in Geneva today.

Action poetry became a process whereby the people of Geneva made meaning from the poetry on public billboards. It began a shared public discussion of the value of poetry, art, civic pride, and much more. This is how Francois Tochon conceived of the school curriculum and the nature of teaching and learning. In action poetry, performance produces a metaphoric message, which may take a narrative dimension. Action, which before all else is abstract, erects a set of values into a set or metaphoric symbols. These values cannot be separated from the context and the field of action, and yet they represent the poetic sign as a means of reaching beyond the symbolic connections usually promoted by the city. Through poetry, the city appeared to be refigured and rejuvenated.

Our Translucent Walls

A growing body of evidence from the classroom, coupled with emerging research in cognitive psychology and neuroscience, is lending insight into how people learn. But how we teach has not changed much. Too often, faculty members teach according to habits and hunches. Graduate students pursuing their doctorates get little or no training in how students learn. When these graduate students leave the university, they might think about the content they want students to learn, but not the cognitive capabilities they want them to develop. Any attempt at a new form of curriculum theory should begin where our imaginations find an idea or concept which, at that time and place, can become actionable in the way I have described it. The scale of the social problems we face is illustrated by India, where schools and teachers are in such short supply that conventional efforts to educate are bound to fail. Currently, over 120 million Indian children do not go to school, according to Mitra (2006), because they have none to go to. Making up that deficit would require tripling the number of schools and teachers. There is not enough money to do this, nor enough time. The problem is just too large to solve with traditional linear methods.

Mitra's (2006) research convinced him that children can learn on their own and that education is a self-organizing system, a concept he borrowed from physics. A self-organizing system is one in which the system structure appears without explicit intervention from outside the system. The behavior within this system is often unexpected and surprising, what he has called emergence.

Self-organizing systems are something not previously observed. An example is found when in his *The Hole in the Wall* research where a Tamil-speaking child refers to the "replication of the DNA molecule." It's emergent. It happens from within the system. Mitra argued that this suggests that children are able to teach themselves how to learn from computers.

It seems clear from Mitra's (2010) work that children can invent their own pedagogy. He learned that children can learn by themselves and also invent the pedagogy. Contrast this with the conventional classroom in which the teacher constructs the pedagogy and the children are passive recipients. It is here that the role of the teacher needs to be rethought and where Mitra's work is exciting and surprising. What research on this topic needs is the kind of foundational structure I am suggesting in this book.

If Mitra is right, then we cannot force a self-organizing system to do anything, but we can attend to how students learn. This, I argue, calls for a complete rethinking of who teaches and how they learn to teach. These experiments oblige us, as teachers, to re-examine our expectations of pupils. After all, what we expect and test for may be lower than what children expect of themselves and it revisits the question of the curriculum. What should schools be teaching children?

Circling Thoughts

Kermode (1980) wrote about the difficulty of finding only the "real" meaning of a piece of literature and he conjectured that the idea of deconstructing text might be very appealing. Stories have become the way in which we create meaning and connectedness. What we have often referred to in ordinary language as "logical" or "rational" thinking in fact comes under the general heading of scientific thought. Most of us were taught in school to form a hypothesis, then test it or torture it, as Bacon would have said to surrender a conclusion.

These conclusions, if the results were consistent, could eventually form the basis of a truth claim. Throughout all of this it was assumed that a general theory of causality applied. However, since the 1960s it has become clear that the theory of narrative has become a fundamental way that we have come to know ourselves, as well as others. Just as we learned to deconstruct literature, we have also learned that "text" can mean more than a printed document, for example turning on the television today yields innumerable stories.

Cyber What?

The term "cybernetics" was first used by Wiener (1994) in reference to the entire field of communication theory. I think this is the theoretical basis of Mitra's work and worth a bit of time and effort to consider at this point. Cybernetics theorizes that a system is holistic and cannot be reduced to its parts without altering its pattern. Systems are self-regulating and stabilize themselves through negative feedback loops. I have characterized this process in terms of re-enacting, as-ifing, and circling.

Cybernetic systems, like historical narratives, respond to information and are self-organizing. In these cases, the system searches for and encodes new patterns with which to operate. Over time, changes in the overall system may emerge in this way through positive feedback. A classroom becomes a holistic system in the same way where each individual comes to make sense of what is happening by as-ifing.

In a cybernetic epistemological model each sees the other and the self through their own set of past experiences, while trying to maintain a whole. Collingwood (1946) referred to this as the inside and outside of ideas, each concerned with maintaining an internal, or personal, balance of predefined expectations and goals.

It may be symmetry

Bateson (1972) was one of the first scholars to appreciate that the patterns of organization and relational symmetry evident in all living systems are indicative of mind. By mind, I refer you to Collingwood's thinking that mind is comprised of absolute presuppositions. For Mitra, this might be that thinking is a series of emerging phenomenon. For Marx, Hegel, Kant, and others it was the historical nature of thought. Bateson realized that it is the process of mind that forms this basis. For my purposes, I want to draw your attention to cybernetics as an epistemology, because this insight helps to glue theory to praxis in this book. Cybernetics for Bateson, semiotics for Kress, Mitra's self-organization, and Collingwood's theory of historical thinking are all means of knowing what sort of world this is and the limitations of what can be known. Bateson, like Collingwood before him, proposed that we consider epistemology as an overarching discipline of the natural sciences, including the social and behavioral sciences; a meta-science whose parameters extend to include the science of mind in the widest sense of the word.

What Tochon and Mitra have uncovered are two aspects of an emerging paradigm. First, each student uses technology uniquely and each perceives, decodes, organizes, and translates information according to their own set of presuppositions. Second, cybernetics may indicate that making meaning may be a self-organizing system inherent in the discourses of social media.

I'm circling back and around with you to keep these strands and threads in your vision. There are many and they can be inter-connected or stand alone, if you perceive the world in that way. My argument is that theory is very much a personal issue when it pertains to matters like this. What is crucial is that we are explicit about why we think the way we do and how we construct meaning. This is the magic of social networking to me, but I doubt it has been made explicit. It's another example of a self-organizing system at work. My task is to lay out the presuppositions, the strands and threads, for you to play with. This isn't a matter of either/or. Instead, the theoretical perspective that I'm suggesting allows you to weave your own quilt, with the provision that what you construct can be scrutinized, discussed, and negotiated. Seen in this way, there are many paths, each based in individual expressions, beliefs, and experiences. Each is a cautionary tale, but not sufficient on its own.

Viewed in this way, learning is a dialogical process in which the teacher's primary role is one of establishing contexts wherein the students may effectively perceive and assimilate new information. Education on this account is an excellent example of a self– organizing system, and thinking of it in this way may be helpful.

Transposing to a New Enlightenment

Tapscott (1998) and a host of other thinkers to whom I have previously referred make a strong case that students are indeed changing. As Johnson (2010) put it, we need a new Enlightenment. I argue that we are in the middle of discovering what that paradigm is and that schools are central to this process and discovery. This is most visible in online learning and Wikipedia, both of which invite teachers and learners to uncover information that was not available just a few decades ago. As a result, constructing a response becomes both personal and self-reflective. The effect is to lay open the deficiencies in the current top-down linear system, and to make it explicit that students are the change force. The result is that conventional teaching approaches are ineffective.

The academic lecture is a tool, first implemented by Socratic means, designed to transfer information from an expert to a learner who lacks knowledge in the field. It assumes that there is a metaphorical cave where truth can be found and that the teacher's role is to be the archaeologist. Lectures set up a dynamic in which students passively receive information that they quickly forget, unless it can be tested or used in a practical manner.

In schooling, we confuse this issue by assuming that by teaching to a test and measuring the outcome of memorized data, we have proved that we know something. It's just not so for anything that requires higher order thinking skills. After a test, students walk out with a false sense of security, having not faced any of their misconceptions. Their so-called knowledge has not been cross-examined as to why or how they think what they do. Today Twitter, Facebook, and other sites offer teachers and learners the opportunity to collaborate in the process of making meaning from what they learn together, to ask questions, to extract knowledge, and to apply it in a new context.

There are other ways to get students to truly learn. Inviting students to explain concepts or to teach one another the material they have just learned are effective. Writing is often an effective pedagogical tool. Another method is to invite students to identify outstanding questions or relevant areas of their reading that have been left unexplored.

And so, to Write

Writing is also more than a means of conveying content. It is a core skill that I hope my students will carry with them. Students are often trained to write in jargon-heavy language that obscures rather than reveals the underlying ideas. Pinker (2007) draws an analogy to teaching here, saying that obtuse writing and poor teaching both reflect what he called the "curse of knowledge."

Having this curse means that a writer or professor often assumes knowledge the reader or student does not have. More importantly, the writer or teacher usually forgets that the reader or student is struggling to learn the material for the first time. Pinker is right that it's often hard for teachers to remember that when they were a student, they too struggled to uncover meaning in a lecture. Coupled together, the effect is both bad writing and bad teaching.

Polymodal Discoursing

For my purposes in this book, it is imperative to remember that every word has a history. Gleick (2011) wrote about information and argued that it is more than just the contents of our overflowing libraries and Web servers. It's a grand narrative, which was pinpointed by Shannon (1948) when he argued that communication was purely a matter of sending a message over a noisy channel so that someone else could recover it. Whether the message was meaningful, he said, was "irrelevant to the engineering problem." Shannon transformed "information" from a term associated with requests to telephone operators to common intellectual discourse. Scientists in many fields were soon speaking of information without any sense of metaphor. Physicists began to think of information as the substance from which everything else in the universe derives.

Today, knowledge isn't simply information that has been vetted and made comprehensible. Any word, any term, elicits a flood of hits. The trick is to weave the multiplicity of meanings, the flood of information, into a discourse that can be shared and negotiated for meaning. Opening this portal is the beginning of your trip to a new paradigm and a different set of presuppositions. This might be called polymodal discoursing.

Shifts in authority and changes in the shape and form of discourses including gestures, music, and art alter the shape and scope of knowledge. Social semiotics not only draws attention to the many kinds of meanings, but also to the fact, as Kress (2003) explained, that "meanings always relate to specific societies and their cultures, and to the meanings of the members of those cultures" (p. 196). Tochon made this point nicely in his work: signs have the ability to offer the cautionary meanings that the makers of the signs wished to make.

These are Polymodal Possibilities

Ricoeur (2005) believed that all self-understanding is derived by reading and reflecting about the great literary traditions as interactions between recognition of the self and of the other. I want to add to this the action of discourse in all its facets. It is the constant critical juxtaposing of the polymodal possibilities that underlies the action of understanding and making meaning.

As long as contemporary society is so focused on test results based upon only one way of seeing the world, our current social problems will remain. As educators, we need to attend to the shifting strands of the world about us. This process calls for work to be defined as an ongoing process. Linguistic interpretation means reading critically the signs that surround us, the signs that direct our understanding of the past and meaning in our lives. Knowing the past is not as simple a matter as memorizing dates, nor is recognizing the self and the other. Our ability to see the world in this way, and to function in-between how I make sense of the world and how you make sense of it, is what makes us capable of learning in a manner that brings us into the world.

Shifts and Sifts

I want to circle back again. In the first chapter, I referred to what Gadamer (1985) called hermeneutics. This is an attempt to create and recover meaning that is based upon individual action and understanding. He argued that human understanding should be productive and based upon questions which originate with the knower. If this is correct, then our curricula should be a process of constantly interchanging cautionary tales through which both teachers and learners are deeply committed.

This fits nicely at this point because I see this, like Gadamer (1977) as "an inexhaustible source of possibilities of meaning" (p. xix). For our purposes this is significant, because it introduces the teacher to the possibility that there may be more than one interpretation of the way in which his or her lessons are being understood.

It also introduces to the learner the possibility that there may be more than one correct way to interpret what is being taught. In both teaching and learning, the hermeneutic approach is constructed as a negotiated conversation that results in a variety of possible outcomes, not a single textbook style response. Thus, the hermeneutic position is transformative and the goal is self-actualization for both teacher and learners.

To As-if

I wonder how in our decentered and fractured postmodern world any such understanding is possible. Can we, for example, discuss in class what it means to be happy? Can we discuss why it is good to be honest or responsible? This book suggests that we can have these conversations and that the answer lies in "as-ifing," making meaning and understanding a series of multiple possibilities. Each of us has been brought up in society with a set of relative presuppositions about the way things work and what things mean. This net of presuppositions acts as a filter that sets the limits of social knowledge and ideas, and the limits of what is and what is not possible.

This is one of the presuppositions about education. We frame each and every human mind we teach, and because all the ideas in the world can't be taught in our classrooms, we as teachers and citizens take on the responsibility of making a selection of which facts to teach and which to leave out. If we choose only those presuppositions that frame us, then we put in peril a hermeneutic process in our classrooms. On the other hand, if we open up our curricula to all ideas, the result would be chaos.

Cautionary tales, conversations between teachers and learners about the possibilities of how facts, ideas, and concepts can be understood, can work if it is in reference to the contextual frames and personal values of our students. This is the process we are seeking to establish, and this is the type of understanding that we are attempting to describe.

Other Keys, Other Voices

All our cautionary tales need to be recognized as polyphonic narratives whether they are sung, displayed on body parts, or written in diverse print forms of poetry, drama, film novel, or historical accounts. This list has no real end. What they share is what MacIntyre (1984) terms "the unity of life." They, in their own way, represent a serious attempt to describe one's view of human experience. As Bruner (1986) said, they lead us to consider narratives as the structuring of experience in a particular way; to structure it in a manner that gives form to content and the continuity of life.

Our polymodal possibilities allow us to perceive epistemological gaps not recognized in the more structured, modernist world. This theoretical construct looked for a map of meaning with unilingual signposts. Our map is strewn with signs of different colors and shapes in various textual formats, which we presuppose or "as-if" to have meaning. Schama's (1995) *Landscape and Memory* refers to the power of place and imagination in a young boy's mind as he re-enacts the past.

The idea of place, with its deeply embedded historical and mythical codes, influences our perceptions of ourselves as teachers and learners and our place in the world. As an example, one wonders how the concepts of "house" and "school" play important and formative roles in our collective memories (Rose & Griffith, 2003). The word "house," both as a structure and as a location, is an integral part of the origins of locating place and it is tied to our conception of architecture.

Seen in this way, Proust and the origins of the self are part of the house and the countryside of Combrey. Both French artist Villemard and American artist Mike Kelly used "house" and "school" to image isolation and vulnerability (Rose & Griffith, 2003). Before you, as the teacher, can understand the discourse community of the students, you first must understand place as it relates to the position and identity of each of your students.

Perhaps it's also about our lack of cooperation. Our educational system is generally of the leadership theory that we should all pull together for the good of the leader. The trouble is that by doing so we isolate ourselves from each other, so that working together becomes a competition.

Aoki (1988) argued for a kinder, caring world where empathy becomes the basis for teaching and learning, and I share that sentiment. Finland is not the only country where this strand is an explicit presupposition. However, as things now stand we will have to reconstruct this based on Dewey and a new vision of progressivism.

We have a Problem

Standardization in school curricula and the related tests of performance has emerged as a major factor in our decisions about all aspects of curriculum. This is disadvantageous for all children, but particularly for those children living in poor areas. The point is that the more education is standardized, the less room there is for providing education on the local language, culture, history, and environment of our students. And this, in turn, means that children grow up to either reject education or they reject their home and its culture as being "second rate." For many poor children, "exit" is the choice.

A curriculum that is rich in place and possibilities is essential to poor children who already start school at a disadvantage. The imagination of children is often fed by reading or listening to the stories of Homer, the Grimm brothers, or Dr. Seuss, to name a few. It is this wonderful, imaginative world that allows children to construct what might happen or to act "as-if" it were possible to live in Never Land.

While studies show that poor children are read to at home more now than in the previous decade, they are still not read to by those who care for them as much as more affluent children. While children may arrive at school at the same age and be placed in the same grade, they do not all begin with the same advantages and experiences. Clearly, factors such as diversity, place, and social status need to be addressed if we want all our children to have a curriculum of possibilities.

It's time to knit these threads loosely together into a coat that can fit any size and can represent any style. I don't have a pattern or a map, but rather a sense of how this might work. So, I'm going to have to ask for help in knitting the threads, in stitching the strands together into a theoretical construct. My book becomes your book, and so the process goes.

OCCUPY EDUCATION

I was a young undergraduate student in 1967, the summer of love. By that time it was pretty clear that we were in the middle of a social revolution. The changes that the 1960s ushered in were a reaction to middle class, bourgeois values. Many of us had been raised in tidy and ordered families where father did know best. It was expected that our generation would follow in those footsteps, but several things intervened to shift that. Since the late 1970s, music, specifically, rock and roll, opened our eyes to the power of rhythm, blues, and sex. Television spread visual representations of people portraying themselves in ways unthinkable to our parents. Movies like *Rebel without a Cause* and actors like James Dean came to represent more than a charismatic vision. They became what might be possible, what we could do, and how we could become authentic. Looking back, it all seems so very naïve, but at the time it was exciting.

The power of that year was foreshadowed by the early work of artists like Bob Dylan who spoke and sang in a way that was so unique and compelling. His siren calls were echoed in their own way at the Monterey Pop festival in 1967, where the hippie movement was formally recognized. Today, we recognize that the movements of the sixties and early seventies represented a fundamental attack on the social values of the time and they had a lasting and deep effect on the shape of politics, religion, and social values. As we try to make sense our shifting strands, we can look to that time as an example of a social revolution. It's no wonder that the West's great revolutions began as they did, because the British, French, and Russian revolutionaries didn't use the maps of the past. They invented their own. History may appear to repeat itself on a superficial level, but repetition should not be thought of as cyclical. We move through paradigms based on presuppositions, but these foundational ideas are relative to time and place. What is cyclical and reoccurring is the way we narrate, the way we construct meaning. Today, we look around and see chaos. We don't recognize that we are in a revolution far more profound than any since the Industrial Revolution.

Although my heart was up there on the stage with Bob Dylan, and later Cream and Led Zeppelin, my mind was elsewhere. I had earned my first university degree in history and then another in philosophy by the mid 1970s, and I was trying very hard to decode the very different discourses. I had assumed that what I had been taught about how we make meaning in my social sciences and humanities classes was true, but when I entered my master's program in philosophy I literally hit a brick wall. Historians, I discovered, didn't know what they were talking about and clearly didn't understand language. The philosophers of history regarded the past as a series of acts to be explained, whereas my fellow historians saw options. Explanation was one option, but so was description.

The debate still continues in many fields of study. For theorists in quantum physics, like Lawrence Krauss (2012), the distinction is the marker between two entirely separate paradigms. In one paradigm, fact is determined by what can be seen, observed by the human eye, tested, repeated, and therefore explained in terms of laws. In the other, quantum physics is pure theory based on speculation and description. These descriptions are referred to as unstable.

In my context of social meaning, I characterize these as the shifting strands of a fractured, decentered way of framing the world. I have argued previously that the scientific thinking of physicists like Heisenberg in the early twentieth century foreshadowed this debate, but so too did the work of the philosopher Wittgenstein and the historian Schama. In the past two decades the importance of these ideas became explicit in common discourse, largely because of Facebook, Twitter, and other social media. Discourse about making meaning has migrated from the academic community to the street. School children, adults, professionals, and non-professionals are attending to discourses which are non-linear, fractured, and relative to time and place.

The emerging field of neurobiology is not a buzz word on social media but its work may be crucial to my point. Neurobiology claims that our brain constantly rewires itself based on our daily experiences. What you do frames the way you make meaning. People constantly tweeting, people using discourse in unconventional ways, reframe meaning as polymodal messages to one another as-if they were cautionary tales. In the process our cautionary tales about our lives rewire how we think. These seemingly small personal stories can be described as, but not explained. They are the products or modes of our consciousness. This relationship can be characterized as communicative. It can be assumed that they represent an ongoing temporal process from which can emerge dialogue, intentionality, consciousness of the world and of other, conceptions of temporality beyond that of lived experience, and ultimately, personal identity. These voices invite us in numerous forms, not only in traditional print, but also in our decentered world as dress, tattoos, make-up, and sexuality. The list is endless and so it should be, as the possibilities and personal narratives are endless.

In this process, understanding and text have come to be read as: What is this saying to me? What is the theory of "x"? These can be read as the bundle of complex and systematically formed ideas about a topic which results in action. Notice that in each case the meaning of the question is tied to personal meaning, not a universal. There is not a direct link to the normal notion of causality. Observe also that as people "as-if" they open gaps to explore and know their world by speaking in reflective and reflexive ways in the context of Gramsci's praxis. As learners and teachers together deconstruct concepts such as "theory," we enter a world where schooling, if it is to have any relevance at all, is not simply a matter of logical or rational causal thinking.

This sense of curriculum creates an entirely new set of possibilities for us. It is one where concepts such as community and connectedness become as important as those which establish truth claims. In this postmodern world, learners and teachers work collaboratively to discover how it is possible to be with others "as-if" one knows what it means to be thoughtful and tactful in this de-centered world. This is polymodal curriculum theory. This is a place where our imaginations find the ideas that they pass on to belief and action; where they find the vision which is the source of both dignity and joy in life. The critical study of literature then provides one way to produce, out of the society we have to live in, a vision of the society we want to live in.

Occupy Education

One might ask where theses shifting strands impact the world of teaching and learning in its widest sense. My answer, which may surprise you, is not in formal schooling, administration, or assessment but in the complete reframing of teacher education. I think all of our futures depend on this endeavour. Let me sketch how this might look from a different perspective, and then transpose that to education.

The Occupy Wall Street movement, among other things, is trying to reinvent the banking system. The Alternative Banking Group within Occupy Wall Street is a diverse group. Many of its members have worked in the financial industry and the one thing they have in common is the vision of creating a new kind of bank. Organizers admit they have almost no consensus opinion, with the exception that they all agree the system is not working (Adler, 2012). The Alternative Banking Group has small groups working on specific projects, like a mobile app to help people move their money away from large banks. The focus is to help people navigate through change. For example, helping to locate ATMs in your neighborhood, discovering what paperwork is necessary for changes in accounts, and describing the differences between big banks and credit unions.

The big idea, the umbrella idea, is to create a new kind of bank. Carne Ross, a former British diplomat says, "The banking system is so broken that some people in finance share the concerns of people who were sleeping in New York City's Zuccotti Park, the heart of the Occupy movement" (Adler, 2012). The process is what you might expect from a committed and focused group, lots of talk and negotiating about what might work and what can work. Chaos and complexity lived in an as-if world.

A couple of times a week, this Occupy Wall Street group holds a council meeting where about 60 people representing the various working groups meet and where decisions are made by consensus. The aim is a democratic institution, owned by its employees and by its customers. Its policies must be transparent and follow banking practices that do not expose the broader economy to systemic risk. The belief is that if you change banking, you change the whole nervous system of the economy. Get the idea?

Musical Democracy

The orchestra without a conductor, A Far Cry, is an instrumental ensemble that functions as an orchestra but is not led or directed by a conductor. It is at the forefront of an exciting new generation in classical music. A Far Cry was founded in 2007 by a tightly-knit collective of seventeen young professional musicians who developed an innovative structure of rotating leadership both on stage and behind the scenes. This group has expanded the boundaries of orchestral repertoire by experimenting with the ways that music is prepared, performed, and experienced. A Far Cry has been embraced throughout the world for their performances and for the conversations their music has influenced (Mauskapf, 2011).

I believe that the ideas presented above could be of benefit to many different types of arts organizations, especially those that struggle with entrenched and ineffective leadership. Distributing such responsibility and power can be an uncomfortable, and even unnerving, process. But shared leadership can also improve efficiency and incite extraordinary art making. Isn't that the point? We might then consider leadership as a series of acts that are distributed throughout a group or organization, serving to coordinate individual goals and tackle the diverse challenges facing all complex institutions. Recent research suggests that adaptive leaders, not heroic ones, effect change. That takes an incredible amount of trust and hard work, but the potential payoff is well worth it. The Orpheus Chamber Orchestra has utilized a shared leadership model for nearly forty years, but its implementation has continued to evolve. The group's thirty-four musicians include a dynamic "core." It is a group not as leaderless, but leader-full in which each member feels a sense of responsibility, both for the group as well as the music that is produced.

Collaboration

For the Occupy movement and for groups like A Far Cry and The Orpheus Chamber Orchestra, this type of collaboration is based on a culture of common, very explicit values. Those values include: collaboration, respect for people, innovation through continual learning, and a commitment to shared leadership. These groups believe that because those values are explicit, structures can be built to support them. Like Orpheus, the chamber orchestra A Far Cry leverages shared leadership tactics to meet and overcome familiar industry challenges. They took advantage of their skills, choosing musicians with various types of business experience as well as one with deeply-held charitable ideals. Now this is something to attend to, as forging partnerships like this builds and strengthens community. An occupy movement need not be destructive. It can be an alternative.

Why Social is the Answer

There are a number of imperatives, and possible presuppositions, emerging for this that can be transferred to education. First, the most successful organizations can turn data into valuable insights. Second, organizations must drive continuous and sustainable operational improvements to reduce complexity and reduce costs. Third, change is the only constant. Fourth, innovation comes from collaboration and collaboration comes from everywhere. Organizations that embrace the power of social technologies unleash the productivity and innovation throughout the entire organization. Fifth, all organizations, including education, are faced with growing expectations for innovative and smarter products, personalized services, and more innovative possibilities. And sixth, social business promotes the idea that new leaders can identify, assess, and monitor risks to mitigate and prevent them. All of this includes partnerships with people in cities, towns, or rural communities, education at all levels, and even government. In short, it's an inclusive concept

There is always a Storyline that takes on a Life of its own

For me, this presupposes one major thought, namely that we invite, construct, and enable face-to-face conversations. Sherry Turkle (2012) made this point eloquently in her TedTalks and recent articles but I want to add my own spin to this, given the context of this book. Namely that it is possible to weave the various presuppositional strands in several ways, sometimes moment by moment, but also in terms of memory. In the past, Western civilization has been a slow and uneven path of evolving ideas heading along a not too direct or certain road to some form of democracy.

Historians, the keepers and readers of the record, have presented us with formulas for making sense of this. To be fair, my learned colleagues have done a good job, but as most would readily admit it's all hindsight, colored by what evidence can be found and how that is interpreted. Also, in the past the conversation about what counts as fact or truth was between scholars. Today, while the intellectual conversation continues, it does so in quiet corners and few seem interested in the complications. What we want seems to be the here and now that suits us. "Conversations" have come to take the form of listening to a rant on talk radio, Fox news, or even the fixed curriculum that we spew from our mouths every day as we "prepare" students to pass a test and not the world where ideas clash and explanation and compromise are common discourse. Very successful people in every field are more often good listeners, and it is this that we do not seem to understand. In order to listen well you have to be able to attend to gestures, dress, language, style—all of what I have called discourse.

Decoding discourse, learning to invite discussion, entails a commitment to discovering what the other person means to say, what their intentions are. The next step is to negotiate a way in which ideas and can be discussed and considered. This is not linear process but circular and on-going.

Turkle's point is that in our rush to keep in contact we are losing this historic ability, and in the process becoming a nation of lonely, isolated people. We rush to our phone when we awake to check our messages. We construct the best possible fantasy portrait of ourselves so as not to disappoint and not to miss out; a portrait as phony as that in Wilde's (1890) *The Picture of Dorian Gray*, where the real you never is on display and one which is often impossible to live up to. As a consequence, we are very much alone.

Schooling is not helping us. Budgets, politicians, and the media remind us that things are changing and that speed is of the essence, not long-range reasoning. We teach children to recite easily forgettable facts, to read sections of books, and to move online when it suits their lifestyle. I love my iPhone and my iPad. I couldn't write without access to all the information that is there, but I do this at as a critically trained thinker. I believe these are in short supply today. I counter the isolation by reading my writing to my students, one in particular, and I ask them for input, conversation, and direction. My colleagues are too busy to give me any feedback and I often have to wait for the chance to give a presentation at a conference, and then hope for the best.

I was lucky in my doctoral studies to be able to spend Friday afternoons at pubs in Oxford and later in Cambridge, where everything was discussed. It was there that I got the opportunity to watch and learn about how people thought and spoke. I was also lucky enough to find teachers like Walter Kaufman who took Saturdays to listen, question, and guide. Conversations like these built my content and they led to further and more diverse discussions that inducted me into a community. Each morning as I sit down to write I have to remind myself to turn off my phone, to quiet my mind, to focus on the task of writing, and to leave the world of right here, right now alone for a while.

On Myth Making

Is this really a myth? Can publicly funded schooling succeed or is it doomed to failure because of its mandate? I don't believe that we are necessarily headed for destruction, but in order to become what I believe to be a successful democracy in the twenty-first century we need to construct a set of presuppositions. This has been one of the objectives of this book. To do this we can't mimic, but we can learn from observation and then move to synthesize our shifting strands into a new paradigm.

No Power, a Little Knowledge, a Little Wisdom and as Much Flavor as Possible.

—Roland Barthes

When Roland Barthes wrote *Mythologies* in 1957, he created modern cultural criticism. His work is comprised of a series of fragments, what he called "jouissance," where his stories rolled on from one to another and where each reader constructs his or her own meaning. Through this process, authenticity is given to popular culture. Barthes believed, as I do, that mass culture is analogous to myth-making and that the roles played out in epics like *The Iliad* are now taken by mass media personalities.

This is pertinent to my position in several ways. First, I hold with Barthes' epistemological position and my reference to education, teaching and learning specifically, is to draw you into constructing your own meaning about myth-making in these dangerous times. Second, my fragmented writing reflects not only my view of the state of things but is an attempt to urge you to take back your usurped role. The role of myth, as Mary Douglas (2007) pointed out, can be pivotal and the myth-maker is a constructor of meaning. Consider some of the myths that we have taken to be truths. These myths have inhibited our ability to have an educational system that not only meets our needs today, but in the coming years as well. These reasons are historical as well as philosophical.

Myth 1: You can't Improve Public Education

Finland improved its public education system by strengthening the education profession and investing in teacher preparation and support. The high level of knowledge and skills of Finnish teachers means that they are able to make independent decisions about what is best for their students. They are encouraged to be autonomous and open to new ideas and broader perspectives. You may remember that Dan Pink (2008) argued that in order to meet the demands of this new century we need mastery, purpose, and autonomy. Finland has put this into practice, and this is one lesson we can learn.

In Finland, teachers have the ability to plan curriculum written specifically to meet the needs of their students using alternative pedagogic approaches, rather than the drill and skill approach utilized in most American schools. Finnish teachers make their own assessments that yield descriptive feedback, not numerical grades that compare students with one another. The result is that students work collaboratively with teachers and learn in an environment where creativity and risk-taking are encouraged. These are skills that we would want to see in our workforce.

Educational success in Finland has been built upon the expertise of local players working together. The key to maintaining their commitment and support was inviting and listening to the expertise of teachers, union representatives, university researchers, textbook authors, and government officials and together designing a new curriculum for now, for the future, and for all the people of Finland. Too often education has been a football game for us. We kick it back and forth in a winner-take-all kind of game. What we need to do instead is to work together towards a system for the common good.

What I am describing is the beginning of a conversation, what I was writing about a few pages ago. It's not a matter of sending messages or staying on top of your contacts. It's about getting in and working with others, negotiating and finding common grounds, and laying the groundwork of reform.

Myth 2: Life begins at 5

Finnish children begin school at seven years of age at the same level, regardless of their socio-economic status. Children in the primary grades play, make music, create art, and formally learn. Teaching and learning are blended into a curriculum that encompasses all aspects of everyday life. It is not abstract and implicit and there is no hidden curriculum.

What drives this, what allows this to happen, is that there is no formal testing in Finnish schools except for the nationwide National Matriculation Examination at the end of secondary school. When will we wake up to the myth of teacher accountability? It isn't necessary to shadow, threaten, and bully. With the proper tools and support, teachers can become autonomous, creative, and productive citizens.

Myth 3: Teachers don't think for themselves

Finnish teachers are highly respected and well-educated. All teachers must have a master's degree and only 10% of the 5000 applicants each year are accepted to the faculties of education in Finnish universities. Trusting the schools and teachers is a common feature in Finnish schools. Schools receive full autonomy in developing the daily delivery of education services. The ministry of education always believed that teachers, together with principals, parents, and their communities know how to provide the best possible education for their children and youth. Except for the guidelines for learning goals and assessment criteria, The National Board of Education (whose concerns are curriculum development, evaluation of education, and professional support for teachers) doesn't dictate lesson plans or require standardized tests. School can plan their own curricula to reflect local concerns.

Myth 4: Teachers won't work hard unless forced

Education reform proceeded because it gave teachers a way to maintain their pedagogical freedom, creativity, and sense of professional responsibility. By allowing them to choose textbooks and learning materials and to determine the best way to cover the curriculum, Finnish teacher became partners in a social/education project. The key to successful educational reform in Finland, and anywhere else, is finding ways to help schools and teachers come together and share what they have learned about productive teaching techniques and effective schools. The result in Finland has been to create polymodal learning communities sharing the latest technology in combination with locally tested practices and creative place-based ideas.

Students from Finland outperform their peers in 43 other nations, including ours. Finland is ranked top in economic competitiveness and this success can be attributed to education policies put in place over the past 40 years. Finland realized that to survive between the East and the West it was necessary to develop their own unique expertise. They chose to become the best educational system in Europe.

The point is that if you don't change and adapt in today's world you are stuck, but that doesn't mean we neglect the past. In business that can mean you are out of work, for instance, publishing or the record industry. Where we are right now is in the process of a massive shift and chances are it's not over. In order to understand this process, we ought to revisit Collingwood.

Turkle (2012) believes that we are in the infancy of the internet revolution. I think she's right. We are just beginning to realize the power and impact of digital learning, social networks, and Google. It would be foolish to think that what we have now is all there is to this revolution. If I am correct, then formal education needs to do more than adapt. Its audience, the students, are not interested in the same ideals and methodologies as I was. My youth was predictable and I could map my way through it. I knew what routes to avoid, what detours to make, and what bridges not to cross. No one would attempt to draw that map today, except educators. Finland represents an example of what can be done right.

One of the factors is historical. In 1945 after World War II, Finland was caught between western and eastern Europe. It was a no-win position politically and economically. A leftist government would be a threat to the democratic west, and an ultra- conservative party win would threaten Moscow. Who would they regard as their market? Who would buy their goods? What happened was that a consensus was formed among all stakeholders and a sense of community was established for the good of all Finland. This on its own is not unique, luck also played a part. The Finns might have chosen to have the best fishing industry in the world, but by developing a social consensus they united to a common target that was achievable and in which everyone felt they could contribute and profit by. They could feel proud to be Finns.

What they avoided was raw capitalism, where common good is sacrificed for self-gain and where to be poor is matter of personal failure. In raw capitalism individual gain is seen as a positive attribute. The Finns strove for the good of all their citizens. I say this to draw your attention to a major reason why we have not been able to draft a national educational policy.

Until we come to some agreement about what we want our country to be we won't be able to. This is an ongoing debate at the present and often a heated one, extending not only to curriculum selection but also to values and beliefs. It is a debate that often consumes young countries. In the past, this debate was bypassed by colonial manipulation, but ours is a country in eternal flux and technology allows us, even encourages us, to make instantaneous decisions without looking back.

Where can we Begin?

It appears that universities need to defend the value of what they do in terms of the intrinsic characteristics of the social benefits of a higher education, and not in terms of its pay-off. Artists of all types speak of the pride they have in their genre, not its direct benefits. That should also hold true for all of us involved in education. While we don't always fare well internationally, we do have some of the best schools and teachers in the world. It's the disparity that is killing us.

There is a lot I just don't know. Not just about the universe, but about who we are. Striving for personal understanding in a computer-based world has given rise to social networks and to search engines like Google. We don't live in the early 20th century where a few men held the keys to the theoretical constructs. In today's open access world, ideas are public. In a matter of seconds, not months, we are free to use and interpret whatever we please. What a responsibility for each of us and for what we are doing in our schools.

We can begin by being patient. The Finns took decades to birth their educational system. No one in our country has that long, but we can begin by revamping teacher education. We can forge alliances and partnerships like Finland did, bringing the best ideas together with the best minds. We can move teacher education into schools and apprentice novice teachers with skilled professionals and we can embrace diversity, honoring multiple ways of teaching, learning, and experiencing life. Why don't we invite musicians, actors, dancers, and business people into our profession? How about paying teachers well and trusting them to write curriculum and evaluate? Yes, we can do that. It's a beginning.

Our stories come to us in many forms, not just print but as songs, as the children of the sixties discovered and as videos, as the children of the eighties discovered. Contemporary children in our decentered world read meaning and understanding into everything they encounter: such as dress, tattoos, facial make-up, and sexuality. The list is endless and so it should be, as the possibilities and our personal narratives are endless. In this process, understanding and text have come to be read as: What is this saying to me? What is the theory of "x"? These can be read as the bundle of complex and systematically formed ideas about a topic which results in action. In each case the meaning of these questions is tied to personal meaning, not to a universal. There is not a direct link to the normal notion of causality. As people "as-if" they open gaps to explore and know their world by speaking in a reflective and reflexive way in the context of praxis.

As learners and teachers together deconstruct concepts such as "theory" we also enter a world where schooling, if it is to have any relevance at all, is not simply a matter of logical or causal thinking. This sense of curriculum we are drawing creates an entirely new set of possibilities for us. It is one where concepts such as community and connectedness become as important as those which establish truth claims.

Curriculum Theory for a Democratic Age

Much of the pedagogical theory that still frames our practice was founded by intelligent and well-meaning academics that chose education as the path for social reconstruction. But history being history, a reaction to this renaissance was soon underway. Music became an industry and politics became embroiled in violence and innocence. Before we realized it, we were all back to making money for the rich and postponing pleasure until Never Land. There have been periods like this before, for example The Bloomsbury Group during the first half of the 20th century, but never on this scale. Its demise and the subsequent war era turned us into a different kind of pragmatic people, distrustful and yet eager for something better, a potentially dangerous chemistry.

I don't believe in historical necessity or that cycles necessarily repeat themselves, but I do think that the past is a valuable lesson in why humans act as they do. By rethinking the past and creating our own analogies we can get grasp our own motives and intentions. It's that re-enactment thing again, and I remind you that to make this work we have to uncover our historical presuppositions and make them explicit. This is a philosophical enterprise, but it is not limited to people in university philosophy departments. In fact, we see it best in fields like quantum physics, technology, medicine, and the arts.

This is why it is imperative to study how our strands shift and sift the evolving ideas that frame who we are and what we hold to be true. It's that role that frames educational theory and practice and it is essential that evolving technological miracles have a central place in this. Educational thought has never been a foreshadowing of where we are now or where we are headed, but it is a good reflector of where we have been. It's important to look in that rear view mirror to see what we have done so we may set sail once more on a better coarse for safe harbors, this time guided by a sense of our shifting sands. This is the reason Turkle's (2012) TedTalk titled *Connected, But Alone?* is essential. It is a good example of the type of thinking that I'm supporting here.

Michael Sandel (2012) wrote that, "Democracy does not require perfect equality, but it does require that citizens share in common life. For this is how we learn to negotiate and abide our differences and how we come to care for the common good" (p. 22). But is the path necessarily titled critical thinking? Are you kidding me? After all you have written you are now asking me to reconsider the presuppositions underlying critical thinking? Well, yes I am. In a 2003 text titled *Critical, Creative and Comparative Thinking in Internationalization of Universities*, Josef Mestenhauser argued that "The knowledge we teach our students is culture-bound, and the intellectual skills contained in it are doubly culture-bound; first because the concepts themselves come from our intellectual tradition, and because the knowledge they process is culture-bound" (p. 16).

This is a crucial point and one that we have missed in America and other Western nations. Maybe it was colonialism or Hollywood or television, or maybe just cultural imperialism, but my generation assumed that the way that we thought was the best and highest form of thinking. Without being explicit or reflective we have taught and transmitted a set of historical presuppositions "as-if" they were absolute.

Although Mestenhauser is addressing international student concerns, his point applies equally to all avenues of formal education and to our society as a whole. What we have been doing is ignoring the historical footprint and doing so, as Collingwood argued in the early 1930s, could lead to despotism as it did in Europe. Today, it is we who hold that torch and the lessons scripted in an Oxford study of seventy five years ago are still as important.

Instead of thinking of international students as "others," we ought to be viewing them as the missing fragment of our reflection. What they tell us is that in spite of hard work, creativity, and talent, they don't always succeed. And the point is they aren't the only ones left out. We live in a diverse culture of many levels. We are different ethnicities, genders, sexual preferences, ages, and learning styles. Howard Gardner is right on so many levels, and though we try to colonize knowledge, it simply doesn't work. In Canada, the province of Quebec is an excellent example.

What are we to do? Along with my argument about thinking and acting as-if our presuppositions are sets of shifting strands through which we can interact, converse, share, and negotiate compromises to construct understanding, we might consider Hunt's (1991) proposition of critical pluralism. This concept does away with conceptual relativism by casting out the idea that nations are no longer synonymous, and instead of stressing difference frames our discourse around similarity and treating everyone equally. We know that the way we are taught to think frames our brain development (The growth of parts of the brain used in social networking is evidence of that). So, there is circularity at work here that could well serve as the presuppositional basis for an educational epistemology and a pedagogy of praxis. It isn't enough to understand this; we have to act on it.

Let's do some re-enactment. I think that much of where we want to go is right in front of our eyes. John Dewey believed that the key to learning was to make the curriculum relevant to the experiences that children bring with them. To put this in my words, teachers must recognize and understand that the presuppositional set that our students' hold frames what, why, and how they understand. Further, Dewey argued that what was taught must relate to society. This might not have seemed as difficult in the 19th century as it is today in our fragmented, decentered, postmodern world, and yet it is crucial. We must be able to relate a child's knowledge and tendencies back to his social past (Dewey, 1897).

Without this Collingwoodian concept of self-knowledge, we have no reference points as to what the child really knows. This points out how closely tied "progressive" education, as Dewey called it, is to democracy. Education is a two- pronged concept, looking back in reflection to uncover why you think what you do and the basis for your beliefs, coupled with the ability to think critically about ideas that are self and community wide.

Dewey thought of schools as communities where shared interests blended with personal desires. School was supposed to eliminate the complexity of life and simplify the context in which students learn how society functions. For Dewey, the role of the teacher was to aid and guide learners based on knowledge and experience. Like Collingwood, Dewey (1987) believed that the only subject that should be taught to young children was history as related to socialization. What we consider the core content areas—reading, writing, and arithmetic—should be introduced as the child matures.

Epistemology was the essence of this for Dewey. The ability to think constructively was essential if we were to build and maintain a democratic government. His views on science were similar to those of Whitehead, that it was based on previous experience. It seems to me a pity that our educational system has bypassed Whitehead's ecological perspective. Today, we construct our educational system and much of our world on a one-sided view of science and the scientific method, when in reality, string theory, quantum physics, and chaos and complexity are making it increasingly clear that our understanding of ourselves and the universe is as diverse as our own experiences.

Like the Finnish model of education, Dewey believed that a child's interests were to be neither humored nor repressed. The child's stage, not age, determined what was taught. This factor alone was the indicator of when a child was ready to engage in learning a specific discipline.

In *My Pedagogic Creed*, Dewey (1897) said that he believed that the ideal school was a combination of individual and institutional ideals. School and schooling was the single most powerful tool for an understanding of how to live in a democracy. The ideal of progressive education was to combine experience with historical knowledge, in the wide sense that I have been describing. Knowing the self enables us to know how others think. Place-based creative problem solving within the community, not abstract drill and skill, was his method. Dewey argued that learning these skills and building them throughout the progression of one's life was the way to build and maintain a democratic society.

Dewey's thoughts and ideas make a lot of sense today, and as we seek to rediscover who we are as a society, this is a place we ought to revisit. Education is very much a social and an intellectual process, and past thinkers like Dewey, Whitehead, and Collingwood laid some of the foundational work for us.

Quantum Thinking

In my 2011 book, *Imagined Truths*, I wrote that ideas about the laws and nature of the universe are being debated. This is happening in a new and fundamentally different way than at any time in the past. Today, information is public. We have the ability to access just about anything, anywhere, and at any time. Less than 30 years ago, debates about the laws of the universe were often conducted in the rooms of the Institute for Advanced Study at Princeton University. These debates had an immense effect, one that I am going to describe in part.

Stephen Hawking, like Einstein, spent the better part of his life searching for a unified theory, a set of laws obtained through direct observation about the universe. The difficulty is that the framework is constructed on theories about particles and substances that have never been seen. This framework is then used to make sense of other things, like the Quark, which explains the movement of the proton and electron in the atom. The discussion itself takes the form of creating new rituals, not just about physics, but also about thinking.

Bear with me while I lay out some technical background for this. In 1907, Einstein proposed a model that is considered to be the birthplace of quantum mechanics. He described it as an event occurring when the first of two entangled particles is manipulated, and the second can be measured without disruption. This "local realism" hypothesis was exciting because it claimed that values can be discovered by the researcher (Einstein, 1969).

It's all Relative, My Dear Watson

Perhaps more importantly, little was known of this by the general public until the term "relativism" became part of our current discourse to describe our society's state of flux. Coupled with this was Heisenberg's Theory of Indeterminacy, which claimed that no mathematical equation or formula was perfect. Mathematics was not a perfect science, it was theory. Although I doubt that the importance and implication of this has yet been absorbed, it opened the doors of perception to non-verifiable truths, multiple universes, and even paranormal experiences.

Quantum entanglement is one of four facets of quantum mechanics that cannot be explained by traditional physics. One of its major implications is that particles physically interact even if the two particles become separated (Greene, 2005). When one particle of a pair is changed by action (perhaps it will spin clockwise), the other particle reacts oppositely (in this case, it would spin counter-clockwise) (Tegmark & Wheeler, 2001). This action-reaction situation can be observed even if the two particles are separated by a large distance (Einstein, Podolsky, & Rosen, 1935). Quantum entanglement has been verified experimentally and holds application potential in both communications and computation (Schrodinger & Dirac, 1936).

The Tide is Coming in

The reason I described the above to you in brief detail is to remind you of our shifting strands. We live in a world that is an interconnected medium exposed by this non-traditional physics. As bizarre as it may seem to you, quantum theorists are playing with conceptions of the universe that include ten or eleven dimensions and conceptions that include parallel as well as linear universes in which are universe is part of a grander multiverse (Greene, 2011). This multiverse might exist because, according to quantum mechanics, particles of matter exist in all possible combinations imaginable. As this branch of theoretical physics evolves so does its descriptive names, so that String Theory and Grand Design appear to morph into M-Theory.

The point here is that scientists of great renown are considering possibilities about the unknown and unobserved. They are acting in conditional as-ifing ways and expressing these ideas as cautionary tales. If, as Hawking (2010) said, "the universe doesn't have just a single history, but every possible history," (p. 32) then the implications about how and why we educate desperately need to be re-examined. What good is memorization, and what really needs to be memorized, when so much can information is available to us in mere seconds?

Shifting the Paradigm

New technology has provided us with the unique opportunity to take advantage of the paradigm shift in order to realize our human potential. Most importantly, we must realize that technology alone won't make this happen. Change is a driver exercised by humans, and education is its engine. By changing how we teach and learn we open the door to unimagined possibilities, all of which are creations of our unique minds, fueled by factors like creativity, imagination, motivation, purpose, and autonomy.

Educational theory is not alone in viewing the world as a series of dialectical dilemmas posed as either/or decisions. Much of educational theory dwells in the webs of the "real" world paradigms, each presupposing that truth is quantifiable, identifiable, generalizable, and transferable. This so-called paradigm is stranded in political spins of the immediate fix, not long-term reflections on the way life has been measured, reflected upon, and framed in Western society.

I suggest that we need to revolutionize our theoretical bases, and for me that means looking at people and ideas outside of where we normally expect to find them. Fields like music and art tell us a great deal about the potential we all have to think creatively and about how mis-takes can become takes. The complexity of science tells us that complexity isn't an illusion, it is normality. Opposing ideas can co-exist for great periods of time, sorting through, reflecting, reshaping, and negotiating, or not.

The mind is complicated, as is life, yet we have tried in vain to simplify it to a series of either/or contexts where answers are quantified in the effort to simplify who we are as democratic humans. It is possible, but not preferable, to construct a system of educating people so that they act and believe in the same order of things. In the past, this was done to keep order in times of apparent chaos. Our times are complex, but we need to work at a resolution of its many parts, not seek a simplification.

There seems no doubt that new technologies and technology-rich contexts are making a significant impact on teaching and learning. Early evidence from data collected at Acadia University gave clear indications that students felt more in control of their learning and that working in groups helped to promote what they learned and how they applied it. Teaching and learning in this context reminded students of their elementary school experiences.

Community

In each case to which I have referred, the community of learners' conceptions are readily noticeable. The more times that people have the opportunity to engage in a discussion of how they learn, the more they seem to want to learn in innovative and creative ways, ways often unexpected by their teachers. As I have said, our new technologies are just the tools, and today these tools are freeing both teachers and learners from the tyranny of an inappropriate epistemological model. Referring back to Collingwood reinforces the idea that it isn't the machine but the mind set; however, the pace of rapid change we are engaged in has laid bare the sorry state of our pedagogy.

Going Digital, Rapidly

Because we live in a technology driven society, quantum entanglement has the potential to enhance digital information systems. Since we depend so heavily on digital technologies, advanced supercomputers are required to handle the load we place on these technologies. It may be that quantum computing supercomputers will come about as a result of ineffective traditional computers. We depend on our relationships so heavily. We depend on our colleagues and our students depend on us. Our relationships are obviously not entirely physical.

I want to broaden that. Crovitz, in his 2012 *Wall Street Journal* article titled "Before 'Watergate' Could be Googled," wrote about a talk given by Woodward and Bernstein to journalism students at Yale University. When these advanced journalism students we asked how they thought the Watergate story would unfold in the digital age, the students responded that technology would have changed how Watergate was reported because they could simply have looked the information up on the Internet. As wondrous as the Internet is, it is not an alternative to the tools of hunt and seek that are the historian's stock and trade, and it does not take the place of reporting from human sources. It's not enough to craft a story using existing information. Information is not factual on its own and we don't teach this distinction nearly or deeply enough in schools. We need to think of ourselves and our students as archaeologists; digging beneath the surface, sifting through the sands to find the fragments, and piecing them together in a way that provides new information and new connections. In doing this we become the kind of critical thinkers Mestenhauser called for, thinkers who reason both historically and philosophically.

Our emerging digital age, and the paradigm that is forming to give it meaning, doesn't need citizens who can only memorize and follow commands. It needs from us what we have historically been able to do, to create and to act in diverse ways grounded in the understanding of who we are and what we have been.

Wasting Time

Picasso felt he was wasting his time when he wasn't painting. Gifted people are often driven in this way. They realize they have a special talent. This aspect of self-knowing is something we need to kindle in each one of us. We need to discover the hidden dancer, farmer, artist, scientist, innovator, or whatever it may be. But if we continue to construct a society built on pleasure and immediacy we will be looking at others racing away from us. Procrastination and wasting time are a plague, encouraged by the boredom of many of our everyday lives. Look around most classrooms, offices, and shopping malls and you see a lot of people who are not focused. In part this is because we have trained people to seek instant pleasure. Working hard at a task in a sustained manner takes training too, and for me that's rooted in finding the thing in life that drives you. Once that is discovered and the sails are set, the other less meaningful tasks can be handled. We can do this in our schools with the type of well- prepared teachers that Howard Gardner and Ted Aoki wrote about, those that teach from love based on commitment, expertise, and autonomy.

This is also a call for our schooling to be a broadly-based, democratic concern. In the United States, we have some of best and some of the worst schools. We must level that playing field. Today, children from poor families spend far more time than children from affluent families watching videos and playing games on smart phones. This happens because parents in socio-economically disadvantaged families often don't monitor and limit how their children use technology. In many cases, they are working multiple jobs and trying desperately to hold their families together.

This digital divide, the wasting time divide, needs to be addressed. When we look at Finland's commitment to all its citizens, as reflected in its educational policies, we see one reason why they have done so well. Each child receives the best education possible, regardless of circumstances.

Who's Going to Win in the 21st Century?

As a competitive capitalist society we want to win, at everything. It's time we realized that learning is not a competition. Each one of us progresses at our own speed. The Khan Academy's success is based on this. With this learning framework, students advance through mathematical steps, some achieved more quickly than others, gaining confidence not just in one field but also in their ability to be successful. Is the fact that the Khan Academy is online one reason it is so successful? If so, what does this say about much of the instruction in schools and about teachers?

The good news is that more and more schools across the nation are using the Khan Academy, and not just in mathematics. There is a lot the digital age can offer but we must continue, as we have in the past, to center all progress within ourselves and our humanity. Like Finland and many other countries where education is prized and teachers are honored and respected, we must recognize that future prosperity depends upon the knowledge and skills taught to students through our educational system. Every child's ability to succeed is a stone in the construction of the wealth of the nation. It's time we found the way to do this.

LAST THOUGHTS

"Things aren't what they used to be," my father often said. My response was, "Thank God for that." Are we in that same position half a century later? Has all the energy and hope vanished, only to leave a tide pool of coldness and self-interest? There's no answer to those questions at the present because history will be the judge, but several things are clear. No civilization in recorded history has been able to sustain an empire. Even the mighty Roman gates collapsed and the tribes from the East tore apart what we call civilization. Is it inevitable?

I don't believe history repeats itself, but I do believe in the nature of human mind to reflect and re-enact. In this way, the process of development and improvement can continue, but nothing is assured. Empires come and go, as do versions of higher entities and forms of government. Collingwood was a 19th century idealist at heart and he regarded this as progress. For me, it's the ongoing excavation of the nature of human mind, and that has been what education in all its forms and variations has been about.

Today we live in an extremely fast paced world. It is as confusing as it has ever been but not more so in all probability so it is reasonable to expect that as change occurs we will do our best and worst to get through it. It's called muddling through and the best analogy I can give you is the Harry Potter series. Forces of good and evil, defined in self-interest and in the context of heroic struggles.

In what I regard as a brilliant new book, *Ignorance: How it Drives Science,* Stuart Firestein (2012) outlined a case for us to consider and then apply. Politicians and others who really don't know what's going on in schools argue that our educational system should be like science, straightforward and empirical, testable. Firestein explained that science isn't like that at all. It's really about ignorance; it's about discovering, in the absence of fact, and understanding, and the insight to clarify something. Today's most pressing concerns, like climate change, are fraught with complexity and we need to develop a tolerance for uncertainty and the cultivation of doubt. According to Firestein, teaching should follow this path:

> They (students) come and tell us about what they would like to   know,   what they think is critical to know, how they get to know it, what will happen if they do find this or that thing out, what might happen if they don't, and about what they didn't know 10 or 20 years ago. They talk about the current state of ignorance (p.5).

So, our historical strands of ideas that frame our webs of belief won't be discovered by pure memorization. It will take a new form of pedagogy, a way of thinking that acknowledges the strengths we all possess, a willingness to listen, collaborate, and negotiate. That's true for both teaching and learning. It also requires that we, as teachers, embody purpose in our mastery of lived experiences and academic knowledge, and then construct a series of cautionary tales so that each of us can think and act as autonomous citizens.

This pedagogy must be constructed in the context of where we are now, meaning that our paradigm is shifting in a way that appears to have different characteristics than in the past. It must be stressed, though, that the written record of the past of Western civilization was also constructed inside a self-serving paradigm. I have argued here that we should not reject the past but understand it, as Collingwood suggested, by tracing the development of the historical presuppositions that underlie the way we understand and make meaning.

This is an historical and philosophical enterprise, as Collingwood claimed, because the forms of thought, the strands of our epistemology, have become more and more explicit over time. Today we live in a period where it is possible to think historically, to re-enact the past by posing analogies about why people acted as they did. Thinking of history in this way renders it a philosophical investigation. Today that investigation includes the role and importance of discourse, technology, and power and those three strands ground our emerging presuppositions.

What I see as imperative is to invite both teachers and learners to participate. This is an exciting and challenging prospect. In our time, the traditional holders of power are attempting to put Pandora back in the box and to restore the old order. On the other hand, Apple, Google, Wikipedia, and many more strive to open the access to everyone. The Internet, after all, can't yet tell your gender or other preferences (unless you let it). Right now at least, each one of has at our fingertips the ability to access more information that at any other time in history. Our role as teachers and learners is to channel that. After all, we possess purpose, mastery, and autonomy, right? Well, we're working at it.

I suggest an example for you to consider is found in the life of Burmese opposition leader Aung San Suu Kyi. This Nobel Peace laureate rejected violence and pursued peace by leading through moral example on practical grounds. The role of a teacher, however defined, has always been crafted in terms of moral example. We can broaden that as a strand by inviting conversations about why we do what we do, what our aspirations are, and how education can help us to make sense of this decentered and fractured time. We also need to negotiate together and compromise to construct common meaning, however fleeting it may be, and to understand that change occurs within us first and then with whom we interact, one small but important step at a time.

REFERENCES

Adler, M. (2012). *Occupy Groups Reimagine the Bank*. Retrieved from http:/www.occuworld/news/7698

Aoki, T. (1998). Toward a dialectic between the conceptual world and the lived world. In W. Pinar (Ed.), *Contemporary Curriculum Discourses* (pp. 402–416). Scottsdale, AZ: Gorsuch Scarisbricks.

Austin, J. L. (1962). *How to Do Things with Words*. Oxford: Clarendon Press.

Bateson, G. (1972). *Steps To and Ecology of Mind: Collected Essays*. Chicago: University of Chicago Press.

Barthes, R. (1957). *Mythologies*. Paris: Seuil.

Burckhardt, J. (1990). *The Civilization of the Renaissance in Italy*. New York: Penguin.

Cain, S. (2012, January 13). The rise of the new groupthink. *The New York Times*, p. SR1.

Carlson, D. (2002). *Leaving Safe Harbors: Towards a New Progressivism in American Education and Public Life*. New York: Routledge Falmer.

Carr, E. H. (1961). *What is History?* London: Penguin.

Cassidy, N. (2004). *Collected Letters*. New York: Penguin.

Chartier, R. (1989). *Cultural History: Between Practices and Representations*. Cornell: Cornell University Press.

Collingwood, R. G. (1938). *The Principles of Art*. London: Oxford University Press.

Collingwood, R. G. (1940). *An Essay on Metaphysics*. Oxford: Oxford University Press.

Collingwood, R. G. (1946). *The Idea of History*. Oxford: Oxford University Press.

Collingwood, R. G. (1948). *An Autobiography*. Oxford: Oxford University Press.

Connelly, M., & Clandinin, J. (1987). On narrative method, biography and narrative units in the study of teaching. *The Journal of Educational Thought, 2*(3), 130–139.

Danto, A. (1997). *After the End of Art*. Princeton: Princeton University Press.

Davidson, C. (2011, August 26). Collaborative learning for the digital age. *The Chronicle of Higher Education*, pp. 1–3.

Derrida, J. (1976). *Of Grammatology* (C. J. Spivak, Trans.). Baltimore: Johns Hopkins University Press.

Dewey, J. (1963). *Experience and Education*. New York: Collier.

Dewey, J. (1966). *Democracy and Education*. New York: Free Press.

Dewey, J. (1971). *The School and Society*. Chicago: University of Chicago Press.

Douglas, M. (2007). *Thinking in Circles: An Essay on Ring Composition*. New Haven CT: Yale University Press.

Durkheim, E. (1922). *Education and Sociology*. New York: Simon and Schuster.

Einstein, A., Podolsky, B., & Rosen, N. (1935). Generation of continuous variable entanglement via the Kerr nonlinearity. *Physics Review, 47,* 777.

Firestein, S. (2012). *Ignorance: How It Drives Science*. Oxford: Oxford University Press.

Florida, R. (2002). *The Rise of the Creative Class*. New York: Basic.

Frege, G. (1892). *On Sense and Reference*. Oxford: Oxford University Press.

Gadamer, H. (1975). *Truth and Method*. New York: Seabury.

Gardner, H. (1983). *Multiple Intelligences*. New York: Basic.

Gardner, H. (2006). *Five Minds for the Future*. Boston: Harvard Business School Press.

Gibson, W. (2012). *Distrust that Particular Flavor*. New York: Putnam.

Gladwell, M. (2000). *The Tipping Point*. New York: Black Bay.

Gladwell, M. (2008). *Outliers: The Story of Success*. New York: Little Brown.

Gleick, J. (2011). *The Information*. New York: Pantheon.

Greenblatt, S. (2011). *Swerve: How the World Became Modern*. New York: Norton.

Greene, B. (2005). *The Fabric of the Cosmos*. New York: Knopf.

Greene, B. (2011). *The Hidden Reality*. New York: Knopf.

REFERENCES

Griffith, B. (1984). *Collingwood on Theory and Practice: Pedagogy for a Democratic Age.* Unpublished doctoral dissertation, The University of Toronto.
Griffith, B. (2007). *A Philosophy of Curriculum.* Amsterdam: Sense.
Griffith, B. (2008). *Cultural Narration.* Amsterdam: Sense.
Griffith, B. (2009). *In the Borderlands of Teaching and Learning.* Amsterdam: Sense.
Griffith, B. (2010). *Reframing Common Discourse.* Amsterdam: Sense.
Griffith, B. (2011). *Imagined Truths.* Amsterdam: Sense.
Hawking, S., & Mlodinow, L. (2010). *The Grand Design.* New York: Bantam.
Habermas, J. (1989). *Structural Transformation of the Public Sphere: An Inquiry into a Category of Bourgeois Society.* Cambridge, MA: MIT Press.
Holt, J. (1964). *How Children Fail.* New York: Penguin.
Husserl, E. (1965). *Philosophy as a Rigorous Science* (D. Willard, Trans.). Dordrecht: Kluwer.
Huzinga, J. (1960). *Men and Ideas.* London: Penguin.
Jessop, B. (1989). Conservative regimes and the transition to post-Fordism. In N. Gottdiener & N. Komminos (Eds.), *Capitalist Development and Crisis Theory* (pp. 261–269). London: Macmillan.
Johnson, S. (2010). *Where Good Ideas Come From.* Retrieved from http://www.ted.com/talks/stevenjohnsonwheregoodideascomefrom.html
Kermode, F. (1980). Secrets and narrative sequence. *Critical Inquiry, 7*(1), 83–101.
Knox, T. M. (1946). Preface. In R. G. Collingwood (Ed.), *The Idea of History.* Oxford: Oxford University Press.
Kuhn, T. S. (1962). *The Structure of Scientific Revolutions.* Chicago: University of Chicago Press.
Krauss, L. (2012). *The Righteous Mind.* New York: Norton.
Kress, G. (2003). *Learning in the New Media Age.* Routledge: London.
Kress, G. (2007). Meaning, learning and representation in a social science approach to multimodal communications. In A. McCabe, M. O' Donnell, & R. Whittaker (Eds.), *Advances in Language Education* (pp. 15–39). London: Continuum.
Kress, G. (2010). *Multimodality: A Social Semiotic Approach to Contemporary Communication.* London: Routledge.
Leadbeater, C. (2007, March 25). Mainstreaming the mavericks. *The Observer,* pp. 1–3.
Leadbeater, C. (2007). *The Rise of the Social Entrepreneur.* Retrieved from http://www.demos.co.uk
Levi-Strauss, C. (1963). *Structural Anthropology* (C. Jacobson & G. Schoepf, Trans.). New York: Basic.
Lindof, T., & Taylor, B. (2002). *Qualitative Communication Research Methods.* Thousand Oaks, CA: Sage.
MacIntyre, A. (1984). *After Virtue.* Notre Dame: University of Notre Dame Press.
Mauskopf, M. (2011). *Far Cry.* www.farcrymusic.com
Mestenhauser, J. (2003). *Critical, Creative and Comparative Thinking in Internationalization of Universities.* Retrieved from http://www.wanderingeducators.com/jmestenhauserlectureseries
Michelson, A., & Morley, E. (1887). On the relative motion of the Earth and the luminiferous ether. *American Journal of Science, 34,* 333–345.
Moerman, R. (1988). *Talking Culture: Ethnography and Conversational Analysis.* Philadelphia, PA: University of Pennsylvania Press.
Mitra, S. (2006). *Self-organizing Systems in Education.* Retrieved from http://www.ted.com/talks/sugatamitrathechilddriveneducation.html
Mitra, S., & Judge, P. (2000). *The Hole in the Wall.* Retrieved from http://www.greenstar.org/butterflies/Hole-in-the-Wall.html
Peters, R. S. (1967). *The Concept of Education.* London: Routledge.
Philipsen, G. (1975). Speaking like a man in Teamsterville: Cultural patterns of role enactment in an urban neighborhood. *Quarterly Journal of Speech, 61,* 13–22.
Pinar, W. (1995). *Understanding Curriculum.* New York: Lang.
Pink, D. (2008). *Drive.* New York: Penguin.

Pink, D., & Shirky, C. (2010). Cognitive surplus: The great spare time revolution. *Wired Magazine*, pp. 18–21.

Pinker, S. (2007). *The Stuff of Thought: Language as a Window into Human Nature.* New York: Viking.

Postman, N. (1995). *The End of Education: Redefining the Value of School.* New York: Vintage.

Ricoeur, P. (2005). *The Course of Recognition.* Cambridge, MA: Harvard University Press.

Robinson, K. (2007). *Do Schools Kill Creativity?* Retrieved from http://www.ted.com/talks/kenrobinsonsaysschoolskillcreativity.html

Robinson, K. (2011). *Out of Our Minds.* Chichester, West Sussex: Capstone.

Robinson, K., & Aronica, L. (2009). *The Element: How Finding your Passion Changes Everything.* London: Penguin.

Rose, T., & Griffith, B. (2000). *Where Do We Start?* Minneapolis: Indulgence Press.

Said, E. (1994). *Representations of the Individual.* New York: Vantage.

Sandel, M. J. (2012). *What Money can't Buy: The Moral Limits of Markets.* New York: Farrar, Straus and Giroux.

Sarris, A. (1968). *The American Cinema.* New York: Dutton.

Schama, S. (1995). *Landscape and Memory.* New York: Vintage.

Schmidt, T. (2011). *Television and the Internet: Shared Opportunity.* Retrieved from http://www.guardian.co.uk/26/eric-schmidt-mactaggart-lecture-fulltext

Schultz, D. (2011). *My Dyslexia.* New York: Norton.

Shannon, C. (1948). *A Mathematical Theory of Communication.* Champaign: University of Illinois Press.

Skinner, Q. (1978). *The Foundations of Political Thought: Volume 1.* Cambridge: Cambridge University Press.

Small, G., & Vorgan, G. (2009). *iBrain: Surviving the Technological Alteration of the Modern Mind.* New York: Collins.

Srecko, A. (2011). *The Theory of Atemporality.* Ptuj, Slovenia: Scientific Research Centre.

Tapscott, D. (1998). *Growing Up Digital: The Rise of the Net Generation.* New York: McGraw-Hill.

Tapscott, D. (2009). *Lament for a Generation.* Retrieved from http://www.youtube.com/watch?v=NebH50yjUYE

Tapscott, D. (2011). The state of the world. *The Economist,* 36.

Tegmark, M., & Wheeler, A. (2001). *100 Years of Quantum Mysteries.* Retrieved from http://www.scientificamercian.com/article.cfm?id=100-years-of-quantum-mysteries

Tochon, F. V. (2002). *The Tropics of Teaching: Productivity, Warfare, and the Priesthood.* Toronto: University of Toronto Press.

Toulmin, S. (1983). Introduction. In R. G. Collingwood (Ed.), *The Idea of History.* Oxford: Oxford University Press.

Turkle, S. (2012). *Connected, But Alone?* Retrieved from http://www.ted.com/talks/sherry-turkle-alone-together.html

Warren, W. L. (1961). *King John.* Harmondsworth: Penguin.

Weiner, N. (1994). *Invention: The Care and Feeding of Ideas.* Boston: MIT Press.

Whitehead, A. N. (1929). *The Aims of Education and Other Essays.* New York: Free Press.

Wittgenstein, L. (1958). *The Blue and Brown Books.* Oxford: Basil Blackwell.

CPSIA information can be obtained at www.ICGtesting.com
Printed in the USA
BVOW02s1911091114

374375BV00001B/1/P